Working with Feelings

Working with Feelings | *Caring for Your Employees Through Cultural Humility and Emotional Fluency*

Isidora Torres

parea
BOOKS

Introduction

I like to think of myself as someone who kind of has their shit together. I mostly figured out how to survive college and early adulthood. I was able to move to New York with money saved from prior internships and was working my "dream job" at Transcript, a creative marketing agency, doing cool work with cool clients. I figured out how to maintain a healthy and expensive relationship with a city that would inevitably spit me out whenever it desired. A double win for me. It was the stuff I dreamed about in undergrad, and here I was, making it happen. So I was surprised when I spontaneously quit that dream job without a backup plan.

Transcript was a newly formed creative agency, just shy of two years old when I joined. At the time, we were a nimble staff of 10 who were all motivated by the idea of creating advertising that we thought was unconventional and appealing to people who looked like us. I joined mainly because the vice president of the agency, Tuân, was from my hometown and genuinely seemed to care about everyone and the work. (If you have ever worked in advertising, you know this is a rarity—especially in New York City.) My first year at Transcript was hard, mostly because we were partnered with people from the music industry on a multimillion-dollar project. If you've ever worked with musicians, or really anyone in the music industry, you know it's like playing Tetris blindfolded. Our main client was Michael, a well-known music executive credited with discovering some of the hugest hip-hop acts of our time. He was hard to work with because, unsurprisingly, when things weren't done his way, he reacted with little to no grace. For example, as a response to a change in an event that we had no control over, Michael wrote me an email with the line "Do you know who I am?" (I wish I could've kept that email and had it framed.)

Despite the emotional roller coaster this project caused, the team trekked on because we genuinely enjoyed working with each other. This all changed when Tuân quit to move to California. Over time, a lot of the original teammates started to quit as well, and within months, I was one of the few OGs remaining at the agency. A part of me stayed because I still believed in the company's original intention. The other part was simply too tired to find another gig.

Tuân was replaced with West, a big-shot creative director with a portfolio to match. He was genuinely a cool human, but I think he underestimated himself and his team. He overpromised and essentially destroyed his mental health in order to deliver work on time. We were extraordinarily short-staffed and our small team constantly worked overtime.

We had just scored one of our biggest clients, JCNickel's International, a retail chain with a massive budget. There were a lot of eyes on this project and very few hands to help. Despite being junior, I was leading the account for the agency and, unsurprisingly, felt tremendous pressure to perform at all costs. I was working late hours and wasn't sleeping; I called my cousin every night bawling about the amount of stress I was putting my body through. In hindsight, it was a cocktail for a breakdown or exhaustion, but every day I still put on a facade that everything, in essence, was fine because I considered myself lucky even to have a job like this. Who was I to push back on the expectations?

I often sent emails on behalf of West, largely because no one else would do it and it was technically still part of my responsibilities; I also usually had no idea what I was sending at any given time. One day, West unexpectedly burst into the room during a call with our reps from Twitter and frantically scanned the room looking for me. Once his eyes landed on me, he asked if I had a particular presentation that he needed immediately. I quickly checked my outbox and passed him my laptop for his confirmation. To this day, I have no idea if he captured the Holy Spirit or if a ghost entered his soul, but he frantically threw my laptop back on the conference table. Coffee spilled everywhere, my laptop may or may not have cracked, I can't even remember, but at that moment, in complete exasperation, I stood up with tears in my eyes, walked out of the office, and simply said, "I just have to go." Did I mention that we were still on a call while this was happening? Thank God we were on mute, but I've never felt more embarrassed.

I apologized for the spilled coffee, knowing it wasn't my fault. I felt ashamed, sad, and exhausted. Social norms told me never to cry at work or, at the very least, never let anyone else see me cry at work; but here I was, crying and sniffling while cleaning up spilled coffee. Then I stood up and exited the office. I still have no idea what compelled me to just leave.

I think about that day every now and then and wonder if I should've stayed. Would it have been received differently? Would I have appeared more confident than I felt? Even if I felt bold in leaving, I worried what my managers thought of me.

I recall feelings of anguish, disappointment, and sadness for quitting spontaneously, but I also felt relief. When I came back to the office to gather my things the following day, all of my colleagues empathized. If they thought what I did was stupid, they didn't say it to my face. If anything, I felt less judgment than I anticipated. I expected to feel pitied or, even worse, like I was not able to "handle" the pressure.

While I had shared my feelings of frustration with some coworkers, I wasn't as transparent about them with my manager. I didn't lie per se, but I did omit some of those frustrations. I feared my manager would've thought I'd given up—that I wasn't the strong team player I made myself out to be.

Employment is central to our livelihoods. We spend almost a third of our lives at work, with most of us likely spending more time talking with colleagues than our friends and family. This was certainly the case for my parents.

Like many adults, I learned a lot of my own emotional development from my parents. They modeled how I thought people should behave at work. My dad worked 16-hour days as a nursing assistant in various care homes, and my mom worked long hours as a registered nurse at the local psychiatric hospital. Their jobs were physically grueling and demanded their attention, and they had to display a variety of emotions as they were, of course, taking care of patients.

I remember at a young age joining my mom at work and watching her tend to several patients. Since it was a psychiatric hospital, each patient was managed differently from the next. One moment, my mom would act stern, and the next, she would be so soft, almost as if talking to a child. I rarely ever heard my parents speak of the emotional toll of their jobs. It wasn't that they didn't emote generally, they just didn't have the emotional fluency—the language we use to talk about emotions—to be able to recognize what feelings at work meant for them. After all, they were two immigrants who were starting to build a new life in the United States. They just felt grateful to have jobs to call their own. Why mess up their futures over feelings? Assimilation and the "American way" taught them to keep their heads down and work hard. This approach to emotions at work (i.e., trying not to show them), layered with their cultural upbringing, set the path to how they would continue to view and think about feelings.

If there was one thing my mom did not like, it was when I would cry. If I cried in disagreement or dissatisfaction, she would ask me mockingly, "Why are you crying?" I think it was her version of trying to discourage me from crying, but it just felt mean. From then on, I tried hard not to cry, especially in front of my parents. I took this same defense mechanism to school and, eventually, work.

"Crying in the bathroom" sounds like such a work cliché, but it really is an encapsulation of how we feel we must hide despair, frustration, or even sadness in the workplace. Popular lifestyle blog *Repeller* informally surveyed more than 1,000 people and asked them where and why they cried at work. Some of the responses, like the one below, were personally cathartic for me to hear:

> *I cry in the toilets. And it's not "ugly" crying—it's worse, because I try to keep it together and I end up feeling even worse for being this emotional while at work.*

If I can hold it in, I'll escape to the bathroom to cry, but I've also cried in meeting rooms with colleagues during stressful discussions. Our office is "open concept" and most of our meeting rooms have windows, so anyone who walks by in the office can see in. But we have one meeting room with no windows that people in the office have dubbed "the crying room."

I have no idea when it happened, but the bathroom has become the symbolic haven for us to unleash our feelings. I've been sad and frustrated, and sometimes I've even motivated myself in bathroom mirrors. There's a level of intimacy and safety that the bathroom holds space for; a safety net for us to be ourselves no matter the occasion.

Regardless of the emotion driving the tears, the instruction has always been the same: Never let them see you cry, especially if you're a woman.

☞

It wasn't until I started working at a startup in business and people operations that I began to reframe and rebuild my idea of how emotions should be present in the workplace. Not to pull a Carrie Bradshaw on you (hopefully, this isn't an outdated reference to *Sex and the City* or wow, I just aged myself), but it made me wonder, Why isn't any of this the norm for work?

I didn't have the answers, so I started looking for them through the research, interviews, and so much more you will see in this book. I wanted to peel back the layers of the conversations around identity and professionalism already occurring in the workplace, and more richly understand the impacts of race, gender, and socioeconomic status. I wanted to see more of the candid and honest conversations, shared primarily in our Slack messages, chats, and texts. I wanted to bring forward the stories of employees who are often left out of the broader narrative of feelings in the workplace. A narrative around professionalism that, to be frank, is mainly dominated by white voices.

So many industries speak about the importance of diversity, yet we don't hear much in the mainstream about the nuanced complexities it brings to the workplace's arena of emotions. I wanted to get the real deal from those grinding every day and helping manage these emotions. I wanted to talk to both the managers on the receiving end of employee feelings and the employees who are dishing them out. People like me, who aren't CEOs or executives or leading conference keynotes, but who know the lives of their teams. The people who get in early and stay up late, trying to find balance between work and life, expending energy where it's needed most. More pointedly, I wanted to talk to people who are not part of the dominant professional culture. As a woman of color navigating various industries, most of my managers throughout my career have been white. Despite the growing literature and resources around cultural awareness, there is still a sense of cognitive dissonance regarding emotions in the workplace and how that translates to my own relationship with any or all of my managers. I hope this book will help white managers further their under-standing of their employees' inner lives and build meaningful connections with their teams, which may include Black people, Indigenous people, other people of color, LGBTQ individuals, or members of any other historically marginalized group.

When I first started writing this book, I was intent on making it a business book. But as I continued to write and hear from others, what started as a business book became a human book.

I'm sure you're wondering: What's a human book? It's an exploration of how we choose to care about each other. This book delves into how we can inject a bit of humanity back into the workplace to create emotional safety and foster growth.

More candidly, I'm sure you're wondering who this book is for. Is it for managers? All employees? The answer in its simplest form is that it's for everyone. But it's probably most salient for middle managers—the folks who are both managers and employees. There's a ton of overlap in both experiences, and we often navigate the work world as one or both.

As you might've noticed, this book is modeled after an employee handbook. The reason is that a lot of what we're exploring together should be ingrained as part of the employee experience (as a handbook would typically be used). Like a good employer, I've provided the following guidelines to approach each section.

TOO LONG; DIDN'T READ

In case you've skipped most of the introduction, here's a quick guide on how to read this book:

Chapter 1: Onboarding
Part 1 examines the foundation of how we perceive work culture. We dive into different aspects such as race, gender, and socioeconomic status to better understand the dynamics at play at the workplace. This section helps us understand the why behind the desire for company culture shifts.

Chapter 2: Directory, Policies, and Employee Code of Conduct
Part 2 focuses on how we've defined emotion and its context in the workplace. Together, we explore what makes an emotional work culture productive and what makes it lackluster.

Chapter 3: Benefits Policy
We discuss the benefits of creating an emotional work culture and why it is important for employee retention.

Chapter 4: The Catalyst for Change
What can we do if we want to change our company culture?

Chapter 5: Career Development
My version of "choose your own adventure." Good luck!

Chapter 6: Offboarding
This is where we reflect together on all that we've explored and discovered.

Throughout the book, I also include moments of reflection through sections called "Pause and Ponder." These sections are meant to be used as tools for introspection but can also be discussion guides.

One last thing before you jump right into Chapter 1. I know that dealing with emotions, both personally and professionally, can be tough, frustrating, and even lonely. As we start this journey together, I would like to leave you with some kindness from good ole Mister Rogers[*]: "When we can talk about our feelings, they become less overwhelming, less upsetting, and less scary. The people we trust with that important talk can help us know that we're not alone."

[*]If you're unfamiliar with Fred Rogers, he was an iconic American TV host who created the children's series *Mister Rogers' Neighborhood*, which ran from 1968 to 2001.

Chapter 1 | Onboarding

"Well, do you want me to be honest? It seems like you've been a bit disconnected from the company since the acquisition."

I had just met the senior vice president of brand at my new company, Giant. It was probably the first time in my professional career that I felt empowered to be honest. Honest to a white man who was my boss's boss's boss. And that was how my career ended.

Kidding! Hell of an introduction, huh?

Let's start over. Hi, I'm Isidora and welcome! Pull up a seat.

I welcome you to sit at this table, one rife with complexity, nuance, and compassion. The table called work culture. While this table feels familiar, there are nuances in how it is set up, managed, and taken care of. And why is that? In the last few years, we've accelerated the development of the hybrid office model. We're seeing the lines blur between when work should begin and when it should end—leaving employees and employers in undefined territories as to how we should exist. We're no longer "checking our personal lives at the door" but rather inviting our colleagues into our homes.

Emotional regulation and management at the workplace are relatively new concepts. For some, sharing emotions was a fringe movement. Still, the majority of people have primarily worked within office cultures of emotional suppression: more like robots, less like humans with feelings. People and Culture (formerly known as Human Resources depending on where you are) teammates are ushering in a new era of radical honesty, wellness, and feedback. It's a new narrative that we've turned to, one filled with ideas of openness and progression. This narrative has sparked both designated "safe spaces" within the corporate structure and implicit bias training. Yet, when we take a step back, this narrative of openness and progression only applies to a few types of people.

Typically, white men are accepted as being emotional in the workplace. Most studies around the workplace assume a typical white worker in a homogeneous, white working environment. It's problematic in so many ways. What's missing is an integral piece to the more giant company-culture puzzle. This cultural context shapes those other pieces. It forces us to take a hard look at what it means for *all of us* to have the ability to be emotional in the workplace. We'll explore cultural context through various lenses, understanding how race, gender, and economic status intrinsically tie into emotions and how this impacts the way we show up at work.

As part of this unraveling of white professionalism, we're also investigating further what it means to have "appropriate" or "inappropriate" emotions, especially as a minority.

Jasmine, a Vietnamese woman who works at a telecommunications organization, asked: "Is my definition of appropriate workplace emotions based on what was taught to me or is it truly what is considered emotionally appropriate behavior?"

From there, we explore the unspoken rules that shape our relationships to our feelings.

"I feel like I've been conditioned to think that showing emotion at work is unproductive," shares Sean, a Black man managing a tech-focused customer experience team.

Combined with studies and research, we'll learn more about how we talk about emotions and stories from folks like Jasmine and Sean. They will share their experiences in dealing with and managing emotions in the workplace. These are real people sharing the highs and lows of navigating emotional labor and emotional intelligence.

Meet the Cast

I want to introduce you to an incredible ensemble of twelve individuals who I was so honored to interview to help illustrate some of the concepts in this book. This is their narrative as much as mine, and I'm grateful that they were open to sharing. They come from various work experiences, genders, races, and socioeconomic statuses. It's important to note that most of these people work in traditionally white-collar roles. Please note that names have been changed to protect their identity and privacy.

Jasmine (she/her)   Early 30s, female, heterosexual, and Vietnamese. She has straight, medium length hair. She is of medium build, around 5'3". Jasmine carries a certain spunk and fun attitude when she speaks. She works on a marketing team at a telecommunications company and is based in Los Angeles, California.

Catherine (she/her)   Late 20s, female, queer, and white. She has medium length blond hair. Catherine holds a quiet demeanor but sparkles as soon as she warms up to you. She graduated with a degree in mechanical engineering but has now pivoted into counseling. Originally from Illinois, she is now based in Cleveland, Ohio.

Bradley (he/him)   Mid-30s, male, heterosexual, and Black. Married and a new father. Has a deep Southern accent that fills the room with warmth. He currently works as a media account executive at a national skincare company and is based in Dallas, Texas.

Mars (he/him)   Early 30s, male, gay, and Black. Mars is 5'11" and currently sporting a full beard. At first glance, Mars seems rather reserved, but is quite the opposite—he exudes vibrance. He has worked as a consulting product manager at various tech companies. He is based in Brooklyn, New York.

Cassandra (she/her)   Late 20s, female, and of Chinese descent. She has long, black hair. When she speaks, each word seems intentionally chosen. Upbeat but thoughtful, she works at a nonprofit educational company based in Chicago, Illinois.

Kwanza (he/him)   Mid-40s, male, and Black. Kwanza is stern but approachable. He worked previously in comics and then transitioned into public relations. Despite being raised in Brooklyn, he somehow escaped having a Brooklyn accent. He now lives in Manhattan.

Rachel (she/her)   Late 20s, female, heterosexual, and identifies as half white and Filipino. She has dark black, long hair. Rachel appears somewhat shy, but when excited or experiencing intense emotion, she can speak really fast and with passion. She currently works at a tech company and is based in San Francisco, California.

Ezra (they/them) Late 20s and nonbinary. They have short, curly brunette hair. They exude all the elements of an artist— effortless, cool, existential, but extremely thoughtful. They work as an in-house creative at a manufacturing company and are based in Chicago, Illinois.

Malia (she/her) Early 30s, female, and Black. Malia is about 5'7". You can't miss her high cheekbones. She previously worked in marketing agencies but is now a yoga teacher in Texas.

Sean (he/him) Early 30s, heterosexual, male, and Black. He stands at around 6'. He wears eclectic eyeglasses that show off his personality despite his reserved demeanor. Previously, he worked for a popular delivery and corner store company. He currently manages a team of customer experience specialists for a tech delivery company and resides in New York City.

Elizabeth (she/her) Mid-30s, white, and female. Identifies as heterosexual. She has long, brown hair. Provides instant warmth to a room and is rather sly in her responses. She worked at a series of startups and is currently working at a tech company based in New York. Lives in New Jersey.

Logan (he/him)   Mid-30s, male, and heterosexual. He is half Venezuelan and half white. Brunette and sports a beard. He used a lot of sports references that I ignored/didn't understand. He is charismatic and energetic and owns a design and technology agency based out of New York.

Last, I'm sure you're wondering who I am and why I'm the person telling you all of this. I don't have the accolades most business authors do. Still, I know what it means to be both middle management and human in corporate and startup environments. I've been the manager, the direct report, the person receiving the emotions, and the person dealing with them. I firmly believe that impact starts with us, the folks who have an authentic, up-close look at the daily ups and downs of office life.

To peel back another layer: I'm a second-generation Filipino American who grew up in a low-income neighborhood in California. As I ventured to college and then later to New York City, I was immersed in vastly different and nuanced living and working environments. I started a career in advertising, working at big and small agencies. I'm known to be opinionated but I have also remained silent for fear of negative or weak perception. I've cried in many bathrooms, offices, and Zoom meetings either out of sadness or frustration.

If you Google books about emotions and the workplace, what kind of authors do you see? How many are people of color? How many are outside of the dominant culture (i.e., white men)? This same absence parallels what is happening at work. Many of us have not had a person of color as a manager. That in itself presents a complicated and complex dynamic that we'll explore together.

Throughout our careers, we show different versions of ourselves that require various levels of emotional fluency both from ourselves and those around us, and the ability to express emotions effectively. After all, we're humans—complex and layered with varying social networks that cultivated who we are today.

We're in an exciting time where we are filling the gap between intention and purpose—our work is central to our lives and we are starting to dictate how we can present ourselves in the workplace. The choices we make and the emotions we choose to emote all pave the way for others.

Filling the Gap

"If I'm realistic about where we are and how I have to approach the world every day, almost everything can be perceived as an inappropriate emotion at work. I feel like there's a narrow box that employers like to see," reflects Mars, who is Black and gay and works as a product manager.

I'll be the first to tell you that things will not change overnight. By reading this book, your work environment won't magically transform into a thriving and caring one. I'm not here to fill you with empty platitudes but instead to reinsert those crucial elements needed to build a nurturing work culture. While I don't want to put the onus on the nondominant group of folks, I think it's important to see our role as builders. We help fill the gaps we see daily and have real opportunities to change the course. While we may feel helpless at times, we do have collective power. I'm not ignorant of the fact that these challenges call for systemic change—we are under the thumb of capitalism and the patriarchy, after all. The powers that be will continue to exist, but we must figure out a way to reconcile our reality with some of these ideals. Emotions are hard and terrifying. Even if we are comfortable expressing them, it doesn't mean it's easier in the context of work.

What I can say is that this book strives to answer the question: What does it look like to make space for the emotions of marginalized people in the workplace? More importantly, what happens when you do?

I hope to leave you with a new perspective on managing emotions and feelings and what we can do to make an impact. I wrote this book knowing that many things are in flux as we explore and navigate murky and uncharted work waters. At the end of the day, all we can do is plant the seed of an emotional work culture and continue to act with grace and compassion.

Defining Emotions and Feelings

Science defines basic emotions as a phenomenon induced by our bodily changes that causes genetically hardwired behaviors. In the last century, we've relied on the basic emotion theory crafted by Charles Darwin and Paul Ekman that proposes humans have a limited number of biologically and psychologically basic emotions that organize into a recurring associated behavior. For example, when we experience physical pain, we're likely to feel sad and begin to cry.

We teach emotions at a young age with words such as "happy" or "sad" to describe feelings. Do you recall kindergarten class where you had to identify emotions based on pictures of smiling or frowning faces? These visuals are signals for how we start to build and comprehend the meaning behind feelings. For what it's worth, adults still need those emotional training wheels because, again, feelings are hard.

When asked, Nicholas, a six year old, described emotion as, "How you feel. If I'm feeling happy, mad. You feel it throughout your body. Happy feels like you're jumpy and very excited about something. Sad feels like you don't want to do anything, and you just want to be yourself." Akilah, a seven year old, explains, "Emotion is when you're feeling something. Happy, sad, and angry. When you're happy, you're smiling. When you're sad, sometimes you're crying. When you're mad, when you feel mad, you want to leave." What I love about their responses is that feelings are rooted in a physical action. If you're happy, you're jumpy. If you're sad or mad, you want to cry or leave. Those directives still exist for us as adults. If you're like me, you're in therapy still trying to figure out what it means to feel or emote.

There's a bit of cognitive dissonance, the state of contradictory thoughts, that occurs when understanding what an emotion is. Emotions can be small or big. They can be welcoming or terrifying. When we think about emotions at the workplace, a lot of us experience cognitive dissonance around which emotions and manners of expression are acceptable. In starting this journey, I couldn't help but think how we started attaching certain emotions to illustrate strengths and weaknesses.

Ever wondered how we started valuing certain emotions?

In Western culture, we think of emotion as high-arousal emotions such as anger and happiness, whereas in Eastern cultures, emotions are associated with low-arousal emotions such as contentment or ease. These cultural differences exemplify the differences between individualist and collectivist cultures. In individualist Western cultures, people often try to influence others with their emotions, hence why high-arousal emotions are ideal. Therefore, we tend to perceive extroverted people as leaders; they're often charismatic with the ability to conjure feelings in others. As a young professional, I was taught that it was important to be "heard" and to stand out by being vocal. By contrast, in more collectivist Eastern cultures adjusting and conforming to other people is considered desirable, so low-arousal emotions work better than high-arousal ones.

Take notice of the impact of these various cultures in the workplace. Have you ever worked with global teams? Do you notice different communication behaviors? In understanding these cultural differences in emotions, it is interesting that the general work environment encompasses the more Eastern ideals based on collectivity. We've all heard those classic adages of "keep your head down" and "don't rock the boat" as a path to success. However, we also see the exceptions of more high-arousal emotions taking the reins and only being available to certain privileged individuals or groups. The ability to influence is key to examining how the West values emotions. More bravado, more power.

One thing to note: the word "emotion" is often synonymous with "feeling." However, there is a difference between emotions and feelings, and it is duration. Emotions tend to reflect how we react to a situation in the moment. They include a physiological or behavioral response, think anger or tears, and sometimes can be unconscious. Think about those moments where you feel "randomly" anxious or sad. These are bouts of emotion. Feelings tend to be more conscious and *result from* emotion. They're informed and may be influenced by memories, beliefs, and other factors. Feelings are more closely related to an experience or a state of being. Emotions and feelings become more pronounced and nuanced with experience and language as we get older. What is typically described as happy could evolve to be joyous or passionate. What we were initially taught is anger can evolve into disgust or frustration. We take these lessons from childhood to adulthood and apply them to work.

How would you define emotion or being emotional in the workplace? What developed your sense of work-appropriate or inappropriate emotions?

When exploring emotions in my interviews, the list of "inappropriate" workplace emotions was exhaustive. Rachel, a technical writer turned quality assurance engineer, described inappropriate emotions as "irritation, anxiety, frustration, disappointment, dislike, and burnout."

When asked why, the circumstances varied but were present in every work situation. When asked about appropriate work emotions, Rachel came up short in her experiences, except in her current role with her manager. "I am fortunate that I get to be candid with my manager and can share my feelings. But, every time I do, I want to make sure I'm bringing solutions to overcome whatever challenge I'm going through. I never want to come off as ranting."

For others, the list of appropriate work emotions was also relatively short. Emotions such as happiness and, to an extent, anger were regarded as expected emotions in the workplace.

As a Filipino woman, I conditioned myself early on in life to regard obedience as key to success. So anything that would disrupt success was inappropriate. It was either stay pleasant and likable or present nothing at all. Mars described every emotion as technically appropriate. "The ideal work environment doesn't have inappropriate emotions. I struggle with the idea that emotions can be inappropriate because it's a human feeling to respond to whatever is happening to you. I think there are inappropriate ways to express emotion, but I can't look at someone and say you can't feel that way."

Bradley, a Black media account executive, feels similar, asking: "Can you separate appropriate and inappropriate emotions? We're all just humans. You're effectively asking someone to come to work every day and be themselves, but you know not like that. But by my standards, I'm allowed to be annoyed. I'm allowed to be frustrated. I am not allowed to be angry. Not allowed to respond to negativity or return negativity. I think it's a little of having to put a mask on. You must put guard-rails around situations. You have to be a bigger person. Being a minority, sometimes you must go above and beyond to be the bigger person. Be the biggest person in the room."

There's an interesting tension that exists between feeling emotions and processing them. While we may have room to feel emotions, we're not exactly able to process them as openly as we'd like or we explicitly refrain from processing them. When we try to block processing emotions out of fear or shame or other reasons, we're essentially jamming our emotions backstage with the possibility of emotionally imploding. As Bradley mentions, there's a mask that some of us feel like we need to put on in order to thrive in our work environments.

Dr. Gideon Litherland, clinical lecturer and clinical training director in the counseling program at the Family Institute at Northwestern University notes:

[I would say] many if not most of my clients are dealing with emotions at work. Of the various issues that people come in [with], the primary issue is [that] once their psychological or emotional concerns trickle over to the workspace, that's where it becomes an issue for services. There's a boundary for home life, and once that mental health stuff leaks into work, that tends to be an indicator of when they come in to see me. Depending on their psychological mindedness, some clients have their own self awareness. Are they aware of their emotional safety? Safety is not the same as comfort. There's a different level of expectations in the workplace that people have. Maybe they can be closed off. Maybe I don't need to be this or that. Boundaries-wise, whether that's interpersonal or intrapersonal, people have different definitions of what emotional safety is and the type of emotional [support] that they need.

Not many of us are aware of what emotional safety is and what it looks like in the workplace. If we don't know, then we default to what society dictates as emotional guardrails for how we emote and process feelings. When we look at our work environment, can we begin to identify what emotional norms are set in place? Which emotions are conditioned versus malleable to change? Which norms can we challenge?

- How would you define emotions? Is it different from what you read above?
- What kind of emotional culture were you exposed to growing up?
- Have your communication patterns changed over time or have they stayed the same? Why or why not?

Defining Work Culture

We're hitting an exciting inflection point where we no longer look at just benefits and perks as the hallmarks of work culture. The quintessential Ping-Pong table was the gold standard startups used to virtue signal that their workplace culture was centered on connection and humility. And while we can all agree that it may be time to retire the Ping-Pong table, I still don't think we have a clear idea of what to replace it with.

Think about your current work culture. Does your office celebrate birthdays or work anniversaries? Does it host offsite retreats to bring the entire company together? Happy hours? Do you have access to your senior leadership? Do you have any access to your CEO? Do you notice that your leadership consists of people of all genders? Can you bring issues or concerns to your human resources (HR) team without fear of retaliation? Do you trust your managers? Do they acknowledge and respect that you have a personal life? Questions like these help us determine what type of culture exists where we work. "Culture" is one of the words we simply know versus one we can define, and its definition remains nebulous in the work context. We can see what characteristics make a bad work culture, but do we have a shared definition of what makes a good one?

As we will learn, work culture consists of the values that help dictate how employees act. Ben Horowitz, founder of

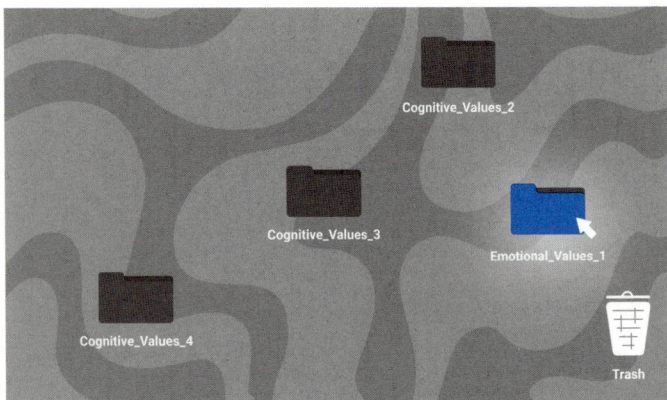

the prominent venture capitalist firm Andreessen Horowitz, states in his book, *What You Do Is Who You Are*: "Culture is the decisions your people make when you're not there."

Work culture brings together cognitive and emotional values. Cognitive values can be described as shared intellectual beliefs and frame how employees think and behave at work. When we speak of efficiencies and optimizations, we are referring to cognitive values.

Catherine, a white engineer, reflects on what she perceives as appropriate work emotions: "I think we've been told that 'crying at work is bad' and 'being too angry is bad.'" For Catherine, the parameters are clear: don't be seen crying or as too angry.

Emotional values speak to shared ideals related to moods, feelings, and attitudes. They govern which emotions people can express at work and which they must suppress. We're all accustomed to cognitive values in the office, but emotional ones are rarely managed, let alone spoken about. Emotional values determine how we engage with our colleagues in public and private settings. Let's examine emotional values from both a collective (macro) and an individual (micro) perspective.

A Collective View

It is essential to understand how existing social systems influence organizational behavior. These are the conditioned learnings and perceptions that have consciously and unconsciously informed how we move in the world. The work environment is saturated with plenty of emotions from anxiety and frustration to happiness and satisfaction. However, until recently, the field of organizational behavior has paid little attention to emotions. One reason for this is the prevailing belief that emotions are the antithesis of rationality. Even though researchers and managers know emotions are insep- arable from everyday life, many try to create emotion-free organizations. Does this sound familiar?

When it comes to collective macro systems, let's explore contextual factors such as gender, race, and socioeconomic status (SES).

Understanding Existing Gender Dynamics

The topic of gender will constantly be part of this societal black hole of perpetual grievance, and it is no different in an office setting. You might be familiar with it, but I want to touch on the age-old binary gender dynamics that so many of us see so often. Whether we like to believe it or not, we condition ourselves to perceive and categorize certain behaviors as "feminine" or "masculine." There's a widely held assumption that females are the more emotional sex, whereas males tend to be more rational. Emotionality within the male structure is often thought of as suppression and control over emotions. Women also control their feelings, but are often labeled as "bossy" or "too emotional" when they exhibit similar emotions as men.

"You don't want to be aggressive, but assertive. Aggressiveness is the 'ruder' alternative that potentially induc[es] fear and disregard[s] social constructs to get your point across. Whereas assertive is the more acceptable version, there is an implied sense of politeness regarding boundaries. They are opposite sides of the same coin. Assertive and aggressive can be interchangeable depending on how you portray someone. As a woman, I think we get caught in the crossfire of being aggressive and assertive," said Catherine.

When asked if a coworker has ever described her as "aggressive," Catherine nodded. "It knocked me off a few pegs. I was younger and a little less assertive at that time. So when told that I was aggressive, it was more of an opportunity for me to back down and think. I felt the shame that's associated with that word."

Catherine believes that being a woman gave implicit permission for managers, especially male ones, to provide her with unconstructive critique. She recalls going to her manager to express her frustration when she learned her male counterpart was receiving more work than she was. When she brought up the issue, she felt her anger erupt as he downplayed her observations and feelings.

"I was getting so frustrated because I felt dismissed when explaining why I was frustrated with how he unfairly delegated work. I told him that I felt less valuable to the team and I started to tear up," she explained.

Her manager responded to her frustration by saying, "We'll get you something to do. Also, when you get older, maybe you'll learn how to control your emotions better."

Catherine reflects, "He just missed how frustrated I was to even bring up this point. To cry in the workplace was a big deal. It's not something people take very lightly."

Instead of potentially using this moment to develop a meaningful connection with Catherine, her manager tapped out of the narrative between manager and direct report. According to Brené Brown in *Atlas of the Heart*, narrative tap-outs are one of the threats to people sharing their stories. A narrative tap-out creates the sense that, as the listener or receiver of the story, you are either displaying disengagement from or entirely shutting down what someone is telling you. What could Catherine's manager have done differently?

"If he had acknowledged my feelings in some way—like 'I can tell you're frustrated, how can I hear you better?'—I would've felt a lot better. He didn't necessarily have to understand the emotion I was going through but [he could have met] me where I was. A little emotional intelligence can go a long way," Catherine told me.

The gender dynamic is still often viewed through the binary lens of "male" and "female"; a byproduct of mainstream corporate America still catching up on gender identity and expression. This binary view is problematic for many reasons, with a key issue being that this perspective tends to overvalue "masculine traits" such as emotional suppression and devalue "feminine traits" such as emotional expression. Beyond the binary breakdown, it's equally important to understand how these traditional views impact those who are nonbinary, genderqueer, and other genderfluid identities. As gender norms change in the United States, it's essential to rally together to build a more gender-inclusive work environment.

Many members of the LGBTQ community often suffer from severe emotional exhaustion from simply existing in the workplace. Imagine having to hold the weight of suppressing one of the most fundamental aspects of your identity. The *Harvard Business Review* described a March 2012 report by the Center for American Progress that showed U.S. companies lose $64 billion annually due to employee replacement resulting from unfairness and discrimination—and many of these individuals identified as part of the queer community. Discrimination and hostility cause poor emotional well-being, job satisfaction, and overall employee retention.

As part of their intention to integrate more of themselves into their work life, Ezra decided it was time to come out to their workplace. "I wanted to integrate my work life so it could fit better intentionally."

With the help of a career coach, they notified both their manager and HR representative about their decision. They carefully crafted an email that explained their decision and wanted to offer resources. Ezra explained,

> It happened a year after I came out to friends and family. I wrote this email that referenced how my trans elders came out and referenced several videos and links. I included explanations and resources and offered that if people were interested, they could always talk to me about what it is like to be nonbinary. My boss and the HR person edited down my email and brought it to the minimum. [They said,] "Only include one link. It doesn't have to be this long. This doesn't need to be a big deal." And I felt very hushed. I didn't feel very supported. It was like [they were saying] "we're going do this and move on." That also gave me the feeling that showing up as myself at work wasn't aligned with their company values. Even though they were preaching, it wasn't what they were practicing.

Ezra shared that despite management's intention to hush their "coming out," their coworkers gave them lots of support. "They were all so kind and respected the use of my pronouns."

I spoke to a chief operating officer (COO), who prefers to remain anonymous, and they shared with me how they've shifted their hiring practices to be more inclusive due to a nonbinary candidate going through the initial vetting process. It took a concerted effort and a bit of rewriting across the board, but processes and policies were immediately implemented to ensure that the company was creating an environment mindful of both this person and future employees. The COO mentioned some pushback from some employees, especially around sharing pronouns, but in the end, everyone agreed to include pronouns across all communication—Slack, email, and Zoom. Inclusivity drives a feeling of belonging, trust, and value, and for anyone who identifies outside of the gender binary, this type of inclusion begins to lay the foundation for a culture that is open and welcoming. Actions like these can set the tone with new employees before they even sign on or step into the office.

While we're still in the early stages of seeing how these shifts in gender expression will impact the workplace, it is vital we keep it in mind that gender discrimination is systemic in the office, and it will need advocacy from all to continue to see change.

Examining Racial Dynamics in the Office

Similar to gender, race and racism are systemic issues that inform every aspect of our lives. Why should the workplace be any different? Employees of color have long had to balance the everyday pressures of work with larger social pressures regarding representation and feelings of isolation (because there often isn't more than one of us), all while living in a world that is increasingly openly hostile to our very existence. At the same time, we are often discouraged, both culturally and socially, from openly expressing our emotions or frustrations at work. All of this can result in much faster burnout for employees of color as compared to their white counterparts.

As Malia, a former account executive, explained to me:

There was a time during the pandemic when I was past the point of burnout due to personal reasons. I confided in the head of my department, [who] I viewed as a mentor, that I was concerned about my mental and emotional distress impacting my work performance. She simply advised me to ask my director to give me a performance evaluation to gauge the output of my work but not go to him with details of how I was feeling. The way she advised me felt like a stern mother, like my openness was inappropriate. I immediately felt ashamed and like I had made an error. She also told me that she felt like I was capable of being able to [balance] what was happening in my life personally with work, which made me feel even sillier for sharing how I was feeling.

When moments like these induce shame, it makes it harder for employees, especially employees of color, to want to be open, especially with leadership responses like the one shared above. In workplace settings, shame is "a painful emotion that arises when an employee evaluates a threat to the self when he or she has fallen off an important standard tied to a work-related identity."

Women of color tend to have negative experiences in the workplace, according to Laura Morgan Roberts, a professor at the University of Virginia's Darden School of Business. Especially compared to white women. Historically, they've worked in environments that have not been physically safe for them, much less psychologically or emotionally safe. Many women of color feel disconnected or disengaged at work, overlooked for projects, and not fully connected to coworkers and colleagues. There's a feeling that white coworkers don't understand, respect, or appreciate our cultural context or journey.

When labeled as an "other" in the office, it's not easy to facilitate a sense of belonging or acceptance. When expressing emotions feels like a liability, people's choices err on the side of safety. Employees, particularly non-white ones, tend to self-edit and accommodate dominant behavior. In this context dominant behavior generally means American professionalism, which is, essentially, coded language for white favoritism. Further research spotlights that most studies around emotions in the workplace overlook emotional norms for minorities, therefore potentially causing harm due to the omission of data.

Moreover, many Black and brown folks often need to code switch, or adjust their language in order to make others feel comfortable in exchange for fair treatment.

"I work hard in trying to avoid the typical Latina stereotype. One, it's not in my nature to be this loud or 'spicy' person. I just don't want to continue to perpetuate that type of thinking. I just feel like I have to intentionally code switch," said Esmeralda, a 30-year-old Mexican woman, on what it's like being a Latina in a predominantly white industry like graphic design.

In 2016, *People en Español*'s Latina@Work study surveyed 500 Latinas and found that nearly one-third feel like they need to dress more conservatively than their coworkers in order to be taken seriously. Depictions of Latinas on television and in movies are also limiting, offering only a one-dimensional view. For example, *Modern Family*'s Gloria played by Sofia Vergara, who is depicted as a sexy vixen with a loud voice and cleavage.

What we've learned so far is that fear and shame tend to be key contributors to what inhibits people from expressing their emotions at work. We carefully craft our work identities to be devoid of false characterizations and stereotypes, but by doing so, are we losing our ability to be ourselves?

To emote is a privilege, and for many people of color, suppression feels like the safer alternative. According to Malia,

> *I've only worked in environments where one's ability to have the space to express emotions, appropriate or not, was determined by where they fell on the spectrum of privilege. As a compassionate person, one of the biggest challenges in my career was feeling obligated to hold space for cishet white men's emotions— it's almost an unspoken part of the job description that goes beyond just "managing personalities." As a Black woman, I rarely had someone hold the same space for me in the workplace. So I went through 12-hour workdays suppressing my emotions, which ultimately manifested in depression, anxiety, and growing resentment for an entire industry.*

Many employees have a sense of hesitation rooted in maintaining a semblance of the status quo. Bradley has spent time working at marketing agencies across the country and explains, "I've always stayed neutral when it comes to showing emotions, neither too joyous nor too angry. There's a feeling that you can't let people in too much. Those little things tend to characterize us."

To be Black in the workplace means constantly feeling censored in your humanity. I recall when I witnessed a white manager say the n-word out loud. My teammate, a Black man, and I were sitting in this manager's office. The manager was a white woman with a bourgeois background that she was not afraid to admit to, think *Real Housewives of New York City* but even more dramatic. Despite this facade, she always seemed well-intentioned and was just fun. She was particularly supportive of employees' outside endeavors and this teammate had just launched T-shirts for his widely popular Black comic book. The T-shirts mirrored the cover of his comics, which were all bold and stereotypical depictions of Black men. One in particular showed a lineup of Black men and instead of inmate numbers, the men were holding signs with slurs on them. I'm not sure what compelled her to read it aloud, but upon receiving the shirt after purchase, she read the n-word in its entirety out loud and in front of him. In a purely instinctual reaction, I yelled at her. Mind you, this was our superior, as in our boss's boss. She appeared slightly aloof and then carried on with whatever she was doing next. My teammate and I stood there for a few more moments and then walked out. Later that day, my teammate confided in me that he was genuinely caught between feeling extremely angry and letting the emotion pass. Regardless of what he decided, my reaction (yelling at her) was a buffer that provided him a millisecond to decide to suppress his feelings.

Our manager could have just thanked him upon receiving the shirt and been done with the interaction. When I asked him why he didn't react or even report her to HR, he said he wasn't sure if he was ready to potentially damage that working relationship. She was our manager, and we interfaced with her frequently. Sadly, I understood the choice between keeping his job and defending himself.

Reflecting back, I often wonder if I should've done something more. Should I have reported this incident? Let's spend some time here: For a lot of non-Black folks, we may be in a position where we feel like it's our duty to go behind the affected person's back and report the incident. Yet, what's often not recognized is how this can impact the affected person. Especially for a lot of white people, it is easy to get swept up in a white savior complex, where white people feel a need to "rescue" people in marginalized communities, but it is important to always keep in mind the potential impact on the affected party. What are other ways we can help our Black colleagues? As a good rule of thumb, don't go behind their backs, and instead open a discussion on how you can better amplify the issue if they want help. Remember, it's not about you.

Understanding the origin of professionalism will require us to unravel our biases and dig deep into our internal microsystems. It is an individual's discretion to do intrapersonal and interpersonal work. I also want to note that it's completely normal to have blind spots or unconscious biases that shape our perception of people or things. We all have them. In an office setting, it's pretty easy to find ourselves distracted by these blind spots. We develop our core beliefs in childhood from the people and environments surrounding us, and they inform how we socially relate to and perceive the world. You can't unlearn your blind spots overnight—it is a process and a journey.

As Wharton professor and organizational psychologist Adam Grant said: "Questioning ourselves makes the world more unpredictable. It requires us to admit that the facts may have changed, that what was once right may now be wrong."

It's okay to be wrong. What's more important is being open and leaning into our curiosities. Of course, as managers, we deal with some questions rooted in curiosity that might cause offense. I recall a time when a coworker genuinely asked me about the model-minority myth—the idea that Asian Americans are inherently successful and problem-free, particularly in contrast to other minority groups. When I explained it, she felt that it wasn't such a bad view and that it sounded like a "positive stereotype." Yes, she was white.

All of this to say that there's nuance in how we interact with curiosity. For people of color, it often feels like the onus is on us to disseminate information—but remember, it's not! Diversity, equity, and inclusion (DEI) groups were created for this exact reason. We'll explore what it means to be culturally competent and to develop cultural humility—the ability to put into perspective someone else's culture—later.

Global and Local Events, and Employee Well-Being

It would behoove me to mention the global and local shifts that are unfolding before us. Thanks to the internet and the 24-hour news cycle, we're living through history with unprecedented access to news at all hours of the day. We consume content about extreme events such as murder, war, and even climate change near constantly, and it can have devastating consequences on our psyches and emotional well-being.

An unfortunate buzzword of the decade is "trauma," and, while a buzzword, it has taken on many different meanings for employees.

"It almost feels like we're not encouraged to be human. Or if we [are], then we're punished," Mars expressed. He referred to

June 2020 when the murder of George Floyd sparked a wave of Black Lives Matter protests across the country.

"I'm the only Black person on my team, and my manager, a cisgender white man, reached out to acknowledge what was happening. Right after, he assigned me a shit ton of things to do and said, 'The right thing to do is keep our heads down and keep working.'" You can imagine Mars's reaction to his manager's response. He felt dismissed and devalued. According to the American Psychiatric Association Foundation (APAF) and the Center for Workplace Mental Health, the impact of racial trauma can have staggering consequences on an individual's mental health.

"When people repeatedly feel they do not belong, they can develop internalized beliefs that they are voiceless, are invisible, do not have agency in creating change, and/or are not allowed to take up physical, intellectual, and emotional space," reports the APAF. These factors may lead to a sense of learned helplessness and hopelessness.

Mars's manager should have responded with empathy. To be empathetic in the workplace is to have the ability to imagine oneself in the situation of another, experiencing their emotions, ideas, or opinions. While Mars's manager could never have understood what Mars felt, he still could have responded with empathy and compassion by acknowledging Mars and giving him space to process the impact of what was transpiring.

"That's the thing. It's all happening so fast. At least give me the time to just process. Acknowledging that alone would have been enough for me," says Mars.

I felt deeply about what Mars shared. Dealing with the impact of racial trauma is not a one-and-done ordeal. It reminded me of my own emotional reckoning at work. At the time, I worked at an early-stage startup called Mansion. We were amid the global COVID-19 shutdown. What didn't help was that at the peak of the virus spreading, the president of the United States made public comments calling it the "Kung

Fu virus," due to its epicenter at the time. Unfortunately, the comments gained steam—causing harm and fear within Asian and Asian American communities. Anti-Asian hate crimes were on the rise and there wasn't much that many of us could do. People who looked like me were being attacked in broad daylight, in big cities and on streets with witnesses. There was no hiding as it all was unfolding openly, and I certainly couldn't have turned a blind eye; there were reports of attacks right on my very block in Brooklyn. My anxiety was at an all-time high—I felt unsafe in my city. It felt like everywhere I turned another incident had occurred—another Asian woman who looked like me was being attacked. Whether it was a byproduct of shock or a coping mechanism, I outwardly continued to pretend everything was business as usual.

As I went through my to-dos, I couldn't help but think about these poor women and my own family. Before I knew it, I was sobbing in front of my screen, frantically Googling the status of the victims, hoping for the best. My manager, a white woman based in Los Angeles, pinged me on Slack. The message read: "I just saw the news. How are you doing?"

I wanted to be stern in saying, "I'm fine," but truthfully, I couldn't because I wasn't. I continued to sob. It was the first time in my career that management even remotely noted something race-based in the news. It mattered to me that she asked. It mattered to me that she saw me. Shortly after that, our CEO sent a message to the entire company acknowledging what was happening. I've asked other Asian women if their employers acknowledged the rise of anti-Asian hate crimes, particularly against women. Almost all of them said no. When asked if they would have liked it to be recognized, everyone responded yes.

My manager didn't have to comment on or acknowledge any of the anti-Asian violence, but it showed me how much she cared about my humanity. The world doesn't stop spinning as soon as we go to work. We are human all the time.

How do we work through these challenging moments together? How do we examine and identify multicultural considerations in the hopes of creating safer spaces to feel?

The Role of Socioeconomics in Emotional Regulation

Socioeconomic status (SES) is generally defined in two ways: objective and subjective. Objective definitions tend to rely on more transitional factors, such as assigning people a higher social class because they have more money, advanced education, and employment than others. By contrast, subjective definitions emphasize individuals' perceived rank relative to others in society. In the context of the workplace, we'll use a combined definition that states that SES reflects individuals' mental image of their attributes, such as their social roles, relationships, behavioral tendencies, and goals that stem from the number of material resources (e.g., education, income, organizational standing, etc.) that they possess. SES affects how someone shows up at work in multiple ways, as Jasmine shares:

> You know someone can easily say that person is just passionate about work. But then I think about my background as a Vietnamese immigrant and someone who grew up poor with low resources, and your work becomes your life. Making money is a convenience, a privilege, and one I didn't have until recently. I work so hard because I'm afraid of feeling that poor again. So it's difficult when someone gives me feedback [because it] feels personal. I'm not trying to take it personally, but my job is tied to my worth and my identity.

Past research has investigated the role of financial status in emotional intelligence with mixed results. Studies have shown that people with higher SES tend to be more self-focused and pay less attention to contextual cues when judging or perceiving others' emotions. In one study, results showed that those with higher SES were more likely to be able to regulate their emotions because at some point in their lives, they were either taught to or learned how to do so. Furthermore, additional research has shown that people with larger financial resources tend to harness and understand the concept of power early on in their lives. Simply put, having money generally gives individuals an opportunity to learn how to manage emotions, which essentially sets those individuals up for better opportunities. Those who grew up with limited resources are at a disadvantage and can struggle to cope with challenging situations because they weren't taught or did not have the access to knowledge of how to regulate their emotions. So when we talk about what it means to have the privilege to emote, we also have to consider SES as it enables an individual's privilege simply because they are conditioned to know how to emote.

And what does that mean for those with lower SES and their relationship to emotions? Those with a lower SES often have less access to resources and, as a consequence, have fewer choices and more external constraints placed on their behaviors and decisions as compared to those with a higher SES. Recent studies have shown that those with lower SES generally tend to feel like they have less control over a given situation and thus are likely to exhibit emotional regulation. In other words, whereas people with higher SES are less adept at controlling their emotions, people with lower SES are naturally inhibited to emote. Rachel believed that her upbringing influenced how she holds herself at work:

> I grew up on a low income, and it plays a huge role in how I am. It's what developed my relationship with money, how I perceive money, and how I show up at work. I feel like other people might have a view such as, "Oh, I need this job to pay my bills,

but if it ever comes down to it, I can get a new job." I feel like I'm always anxious because I need this job. If I get overwhelmed at work, that pressure doubles because it makes me wonder about my job security. This fear hangs over my head, and I feel like I need to be grateful to be in this position. I often show this happy demeanor even when I don't feel like it. To show that I'm grateful and as another way to deflect how I'm feeling.

While SES may seem like a more external factor to determining how someone shows emotion, it's essential to keep it in mind when we think about an employee's holistic self.

Alongside examining SES from an individual standpoint, we should note the impact of SES on how an organization is founded and built. Many startups have founders who are featured on the Forbes 30 Under 30 list. We praise them for their tenacity and hustle. Some of us even covet their fame. However, as a society, we tend to gloss over the intergenerational wealth and access that often contributes to their success.

The barrier to entry into entrepreneurship is a lot harder for those who come from disadvantaged socioeconomic backgrounds. In 2013, Ross Levine and Rona Rubenstein, economists at University of California, Berkeley, examined common traits among entrepreneurs and found that most were highly educated white males.

"If one does not have money in the form of a family with money, the chances of becoming an entrepreneur drop quite a bit," Levine told *Quartz*, a business-focused news organization.

In a *Forbes* article about the cost of bias and racism in venture funding, Daniel Applewhite wrote, "Although entrepreneurs are expected to raise friends and family rounds, this expectation is born of bias. African Americans have an average net worth of $11K compared to $144K for white Americans. With this lack of access to early capital and generational wealth, most family members and friends cannot invest, regardless of how great the idea is."

Marc Andreessen, cofounder and general partner of the venture capital firm Andreessen Horowitz (a16z) argues that people ask for many things from a company—salary, span of control, and titles—but titles, in actuality, cost nothing. So, people will receive better titles for less compensation, particularly in the early days of a startup, but not everyone can accept that trade.

The "like me" theory explains that we tend to choose or recruit people similar to ourselves, particularly in terms of race, gender, and SES. Many founders or CEOs are white and male, and many already have financial safety nets and don't need immediate cash compensation to survive. Many founders then hire executive teams of people with similar backgrounds who have the ability to work for fewer dollars or more equity in exchange for less of a salary (i.e., those who have financial safety nets). The executive team will then hire the management team and, no surprise, it's usually made up of folks like them. Thus, the cycle continues of hiring people with similar financial statuses who can likely afford to take a title over compensation for some time.

We don't tend to see diversity—in either race or SES—until we reach middle management. If you've ever wondered why leadership in an organization might seem out of touch, it is often because there is a vast socioeconomic gap between leadership and management.

For what it's worth, I'm not saying that if you have the means to start a company because you have a safety net, that you're inept at witnessing or managing emotions. This is more about generating awareness about how socioeconomic factors come into play when we think about how an organization develops.

Why is understanding race, gender, and SES of employees important? Because understanding emotional values through a macro lens will help managers contextualize the larger systems at play and how they are framed within the working environment. It gives managers a bird's-eye view of the many layers and complexities that exist within their proximity, enabling them to establish a foundation to continue to build their own empathy and perspective.

- Have macro systems such as gender, race, or SES impacted the way you view the workplace? If so, how?
- Have you ever spoken to anyone else about these broader systems and how they impact the way you work?
- Has your company ever touched on complex topics such as race and gender?

AN INDIVIDUAL VIEW

Now that we've set the larger macrosystems in context, let's dive into how emotional values are defined and viewed on an individual level. When we think about what drives our core beliefs and influences, we often look to the microsystems surrounding us: family, friends, school, social activities, and work. Microsystems are physical characteristics, resources, and perceived social relationships experienced by the individual person. That is to say, who and what we surround ourselves with largely influence how we behave and feel. While many microsystems inherently play a role in how individuals view emotional values, we will focus on these three ideas:

- Work identity as part of our internal construct
- How life events impact work emotions
- Finding value beyond the dollar

Work Identity as Part of Our Internal Construct

Our identity is composed of several context-contingent versions of ourselves. We form both social identities and personal identities in order to navigate and survive the world. With employment being central to our lived experiences, we tend to rely on a work personality to fulfill our desire for belongingness and self-preservation by distinguishing ourselves from others. Emotions become one of the vehicles of communication to potentially help us build relationships with others or make a means to protect ourselves by creating emotional boundaries or, in some cases, intentionally suppressing them.

To put it another way, our work identity is an abbreviated version of who we are with fewer emotions and more to hide because of the environment in which they exist.

What causes us to be emotionally incongruent?

As employees, we can go through a work version of "fight-flight-freeze." When big emotions are directed at us, we tend to freeze up and go through "emotional paralysis." If you're experiencing paralysis, then you are likely experiencing a moment of friction, possibly generated by feelings of anger or frustration. Friction occurs when we've done enough "surface acting"—faking emotions for work's sake—and want to implode with our deeper, genuinely felt feelings. It's the difference between cursing someone out and trying to show restraint when someone does something harmful or offensive to you at work.

As a Filipino American, I was taught at a young age that I did not need to rock the proverbial boat. This mindset was partly due to benevolent assimilation, which was a policy that the United States put in place toward the Philippines in the late 1800s, requiring Filipinos to adopt white American culture. For my parents and grandparents, it meant keeping our heads down. I took that same level of obedience to school and my career. I rarely felt like I could speak up for fear of getting in trouble.

Mars delves into his particular office dynamic, "So I'm Black, and when people find out I'm also gay, I can almost feel how different they talk to me. Usually, with women, there's a

level of comfort that starts. Whether it's because they feel I won't hit on them, they just feel more at ease. But you feel the distance with men, especially white men."

Our jobs become our identity markers, a window to who we are, and we tend to protect this version of ourselves from any threats in the workplace. However, our professional selves are not the only self that we inevitably show. I can count the hours of therapy I've spent trying to understand where the delineation lies.

When we think about creating psychological safety for our work teams, we should understand the various contexts that make us both individuals and parts of a collective. A deeper understanding could create beneficial organizational outcomes and overall better experiences. We'll touch more on psychological safety later in the book.

How Life Events Impact Work Emotions

While work makes up a good portion of our lives, it isn't our entire lives. We have families, partners, and friendships. We can experience joy, love, loss, grief, or even death within those relationships. We celebrate major life events such as marriage, the birth of a child, or moving to a new home, and experience relatively unspoken-about major life events like divorce, miscarriages, platonic and romantic breakups, or losing one's home. We experience great and not-so-great health moments leading to sick days or days where we don't feel our best. We experience so many other life events beyond the walls of our office. As such, we're prone to transferring some of these life emotions into the workplace. Managing an employee who is going through a stressful period is "one of the real challenges all bosses face," says Linda Hill, professor at Harvard Business

School and author of *Being the Boss*. How do we see this manifest for employees?

- Employees who are overwhelmed with emotional issues in their personal lives may have trouble prioritizing and staying focused at work.
- An employee going through a personal crisis may need time off to receive outside support.
- Emotions such as anger or frustration may emerge unexpectedly due to emotional exhaustion from a personal crisis.
- Personal challenges may cause the employee to shut down emotionally across the board.

It's not easy navigating both life and work stress. We've all been in some type of predicament where our work lives become secondary to whatever's unfolding before us.

According to new research by Bensinger, DuPont & Associates, 47% of employees say that problems in their personal lives sometimes affect their work performance. Nick Glozier, a professor of psychological medicine at the University of Sydney, conducted a study on the emotional well-being and life satisfaction of 14,000 people across 16 years as they weathered 18 common life events including deaths, family additions and subtractions, job changes, criminal events, health problems, and financial swings. Additionally, most people don't generally suffer from multiple negative life events (with the exception of a family member enduring a health crisis, which then averages out to every four and a half years) and we tend to experience major life moments in short periods of time. Most tend to go back to their baseline of well-being and emotional regulation relatively quickly.

I am no stranger to having my personal life inject itself into my work. I'm guilty of being a bit too vulnerable in sharing some of my challenges while at work. In part, some of my motivation for being so open was to normalize feeling crappy when bad things happen.

In my late twenties, I was going through my first significant relationship breakup. In the span of one night, it felt like my life had been thrown into a snow globe and furiously shaken. Breakups are tough, emotionally demanding, and exhausting. It's even more challenging when you live together and someone has to move out. Unfortunately, that someone was me. I didn't know how to process the breakup, much less figure out how to be a shell of the professional I was.

In my previous work environments I rarely saw anyone break down because of a breakup. Could I even muster the courage to share the news with my manager and request a few days off? It's funny because everyone knows how emotionally taxing breakups are, yet we rarely acknowledge the impact of a broken heart in the workplace. The following morning, I called my manager and told her what was happening. It felt extremely embarrassing but also relieving to let her know that I wasn't going to be my best self at work. Her response was sincere and kind, and I felt like I could take the time I needed to gather myself (and my shit) together. Had my manager dismissed the emotional impact of my breakup or minimized the pain that I was feeling, I think our relationship would have changed drastically.

My manager exhibiting care inspired others in the workplace to extend the same grace when more coworkers went through similar personal situations that year. (It was a bad year for relationships—a lot of folks within the company went through breakups.)

Finding Value Beyond the Dollar

I was grabbing coffee with a friend who was catching me up on the latest news of her life and her work. She's in the music industry and works with artists to create cool things. We met through an event around music and Asian Americans. If you've ever worked in the music industry, you know that the environment is cutthroat. The grind, the commitment, and the toxicity are all part of the industry's welcome package. I, unfortunately, have had a few run-ins that have resulted in me hanging up on a conference call with a well-known music veteran. It may be a biased view, but the stereotype of music executives berating employees was not too far off from my personal experience. It's a tough industry, and I commend anyone who pursues a career there. All this to say, my friend deals with a lot of shit daily.

When filling me in on her latest challenges, I asked her, "Why do you stay?" She simply responded, "Because I think I'm making a difference. They weren't doing what I'm doing years ago [as it pertains to working with Asian artists]."

Many of us stay in work environments that might not make us feel good, but we know there's "something" more. The "something" can be success or the desire to help other people or even just a feeling of security. For clarity, I don't believe that people love work. If we had a choice in deciding what to do with our time, I think the idea of work would be way down the list. However, some of us can "job craft." Coined by Amy Wrzesniewski, job crafting refers to changing your job to make it more engaging and meaningful based on your standards. Wrzesniewski became interested in testing which employees loved their job, which didn't, and why. As part of Wrzesniewski's research, she interviewed custodial workers at a hospital. Then, the janitors' duties consisted of cleaning patients' rooms every day. As anticipated, she received data that coincided with her hypothesis: folks griped about the job. But it was the second group of workers, who had the same exact occupation on paper, that surprised her. They felt their labor was highly skilled. When talking about their interactions with patients and visitors, they described the work in "rich relational terms," says Wrzesniewski.

"It was not just that they were taking the same job and feeling better about it, pulling themselves up by their bootstraps and whistling. It was that they were doing a different job." One example that Wrzesniewski observed was a woman from the second group who worked in a unit where comatose patients stayed. She made a habit of moving around the art in the hospital rooms. When asked why, she explained that, though she wasn't a doctor, she thought it was at least possible that a change in scenery might spark something in the patients' unconscious brains. It wasn't the work that motivated this group, it was what they felt *after* doing the work.

Going back to my friend's story, I understood why she felt like she wanted to stay. She had found intrinsic value in her job that made her feel good. The value she receives drives her motivation to stay and her consideration when she thinks about how she should act and feel in the workplace. Bureaucracy and office politics do not sleep. For her, it's a constant struggle and balance in deciding which emotional path she should go down.

TOO LONG; DIDN'T READ

We touched on the complex structures and systems that influence an individual's emotional values. A few takeaways:

- The workplace contains both cognitive and emotional values that govern how employees should work and feel.
- Social norms inform many unspoken ways of defining emotions and feelings in the workplace.
- We all live with macro- and microsystems that influence how and why we emote in the workplace, and they're the driving motivation for restricting, emphasizing, or even suppressing emotions at work.

By framing emotional values through collective and individual lenses, we are better suited to develop healthy emotional work cultures.

Reflection   What has formulated your perception of appropriate and inappropriate emotions in the workplace?

- Have there been instances where you've had to check your biases?
- Have you had to readjust a behavior or code switch to appease others in the workplace?
- Have you dealt with a major emotional life event while at work? How did your coworkers and manager respond?

Chapter 2 | Directory, Policies, and Employee Code of Conduct

Understanding and Strategizing Your Emotions

I've spent a lot of time wondering what makes a workplace ripe for emotions. The most obvious answer is that we're human—we're squishy things made of atoms and particles that navigate a physical world—but when you look at other dimensions, like where and how we spend our time, it's not surprising that we experience feelings at work. The proverbial door where we check our feelings has never *really* existed. For many marginalized communities, feelings are experienced in confined spaces, email inboxes, or untouched paperwork. Mainstream media has overemphasized the idea that we separate work and life, when we actually don't. As noted in the last chapter, we're all feeling things at an individual or collective level, but how we choose to process them is unique to us.

I'm of the belief that you have to know the rules in order to break them. In our case, we need to examine the type of workplace emotions we deal with so that we can begin to create new rules (or break the old ones). Like any good employee handbook, this one is divided into sections that will help you and your team usher emotions thoughtfully into your workspace. We'll start off with the following:

Emotion Directory   Understand the modern-day layered lexicon used for describing emotions. Get ready.

Internal Communications Policy   Identify which characteristics can contribute to emotional work culture.

Employee Code of Conduct   Show up for ourselves and for each other with the intention to cultivate actions and push toward a more emotional work culture.

Emotion Directory

It's taken years for me to understand how I show emotion. At the most basic level, I've had to ask myself: What is emotion?

"The only thing certain in the emotion field is that no one agrees on how to define emotion," shared Alan Fridlund, an associate professor of psychological and brain sciences at the University of California, Santa Barbara, in *The Atlantic*. We know emotions are something meaningful. Sometimes they are fleeting, and other times they take up some residency.

Harvard Medical School psychologist Susan David explained to Dr. Laurie Santos in an episode of *The Happiness Lab* that emotions are data our brains process to signal to us how to adapt to a situation. In other words, emotions tell us what we need, usually to survive. For example, if I am noticing the feeling of exhaustion, I can deduce that my body and mind may need more rest than I've been giving them. In the workplace context, the definition (or non-definition) of emotions becomes even more complex by virtue of circumstance. When we think about the workplace, there are "rules," either explicit or implicit, that dictate how and when we should feel.

There are a few baseline emotions we are familiar with—anger, sadness, and joy, for example—but I want us to understand emotions rather than just identify them. So first, we should probably be able to talk about them. Emotional fluency is the ability to express our emotions in verbal language so that we can convey how we feel.

In *Atlas of the Heart*, Brené Brown writes that the ability to name feelings precisely is a crucial skill. "If we want to find the way back to ourselves and one another, we need language." She continues: "[We need] the grounded confidence to both tell our stories and be stewards of the stories we hear." Thanks to years of research, Brown maps out 87 specific emotions—this is roughly 85 more emotions than we tend to think about (by we, I mean me).

We won't go through all 87 emotions, but I highly recommend that you do so at another time. Instead, we'll focus on a few baseline emotions that capture some of the more nuanced sentiments we tend to encounter in the workplace beyond anger, sadness, and joy. The goal of this section is for us to align on the same base of feelings. (Word of caution here: you'll hear a lot from Brown in this section, because: (1) she is mainstream enough that her studies and research are readily available for all, and (2) she is extraordinarily skilled at tying data into story-telling, which makes digesting information so much easier.)

We'll start by categorizing feelings into two buckets:

Feelings We'll Circle Back To

Happiness
Trust
Vulnerability
Compassion
Empathy

"Per My Last Email" Feelings

Anger
Frustration
Disappointment
Envy
Stress or Overwhelm

Feelings We'll Circle Back To

This bucket includes generally positive emotions that are unharmful to yourself and others in the workplace. When we use the phrase "let's circle back," it usually suggests following up or coming back to an idea or task. In the same vein, we look at these feelings as ones we'd like to return to because they've provided us with some level of satisfaction. For example, less friction with your coworker on an impending deadline.

Happiness   Hear me out. I know that it might feel a little tough to equate feelings of happiness with the workplace. You may even feel like joy is a better summation, when you experience moments of elatedness tied to a big win or a raise or promotion. This is a deliberate choice in wording because happiness and work don't often pair up, so this is where semantics play an important role.

Researcher Mathew Kuan Johnson explains that people find experiences of joy difficult to explain. He hypothesizes that joy is essentially a spiritual experience whereas happiness is generally defined as a state of feeling pleasure often related to one's immediate environment or current circumstances. Based on these explanations, happiness feels more pragmatic in the context of work (unless your work is spiritual, in which case, please use "joy"!). I'm moved by the idea that happiness is a changing state dictated by factors that may not be within our control. Using this definition, I think we can find moments of happiness in our day-to-day work lives. This can happen on a personal level ("Yes, I finished the report!") or on a collective level ("Yay, we got this bonus!")

Trust   Trust in the workplace is characterized by a willingness to be vulnerable with other parties expecting that their intentions or behavior in important matters will be positive. Interpersonal trust, placing this willingness to be vulnerable onto another person, is crucial to work relationships.

I'm a firm believer that for teams to be productive, trust and chemistry must be present, and most CEOs agree. In its 2016 global CEO survey, Pricewaterhouse Cooper reported that 55% of CEOs think that a lack of trust is a threat to their organization's growth. Researcher Paul J. Zak reported in the *Harvard Business Review*: "People at high-trust companies report 74% less stress, 106% more energy at work, 50% higher productivity, 13% fewer sick days, 76% more engagement, 29% more satisfaction with their lives, 40% less burnout."

When asked to describe how he felt trust showed up in the workplace, Bradley told me:

> *Trust can come in different forms in the workplace. One way is trust in work ethics, or functional trust, as I like to call it. For example, if you're out of the office, you can trust this person to*

take care of things while you're out. The second way is personal trust. Can I confide in this person without them running and telling people what I said? Along with functional trust, especially if they're your manager, I think it's important to know that you can trust them when you tell them "Hey, I'm feeling overworked" and have them not continue to pile on more work.

For some, trust is transactional, that is, "You got my back and I got yours." Yet, in the workplace, trust is conditional, meaning we have to decipher the gains and losses on a personal level (e.g., feeling burnt out) or more broadly (e.g., coverage while you're out on break). Think about the ways you trust your manager and your teammates; was it built over time because of what they completed or accomplished?

Vulnerability   When expressed in the right context, vulnerability can be powerful. A wise therapist once told me, "Vulnerability is a sacred place. Not everyone should have access." Ergo, your manager doesn't need to know your family history, but should maybe understand why you were frustrated in that meeting.

Sharing vulnerability in the workplace is a superpower because it allows your teammates or manager to get to know you beyond what they see on the surface. Vulnerability requires bravery and courage, and, ideally, is met with feelings of openness. These feelings tend to help build trust and compassion within working relationships.

Think about the ways we form relationships with others outside of work. Those same values of honesty and vulnerability can be injected into your professional relationships. A key example when vulnerability is useful (and is usually a tough ask for most people) is when asking for help.

Compassion   Compassion is both an action and a feeling. Compassion in the workplace is defined as expressed feelings of affection, caring, and tenderness toward subordinates or colleagues without the expectation of specific organizational benefits. While still in its infancy as a research area, researchers find that compassion is an emerging benefit for the well-being of both the employees and the overall organization. Global management consulting firm McKinsey conducted research that showed it was imperative for leaders to demonstrate compassionate leadership during times of distress.

Compassion always felt like a big emotion to me. I think a part of me connected any type of kindness or compassion in the workplace to weakness because I associated compassion with being perceived as nurturing, which is a common perception of women in the workplace. But after further reflection, I realized that I saw a lot of "good feeling" emotions as characteristics that would pigeonhole me as "too nurturing." Honestly, it was a shame and I'm glad I recognized it and changed my perception of being compassionate. As women, we are so often conditioned or assumed to be the caretakers regardless of the environment, but we can challenge those conventions. Why? Because gender stereotypes are stupid.

Empathy   Empathy is an emotional skill set that allows us to understand what someone is experiencing and reflect that understanding. Most researchers agree there are at least two forms of empathy: cognitive and affective empathy. We define cognitive empathy as the ability to infer another person's *thoughts* or *beliefs* and affective empathy as the ability to infer an individual's *feelings* or *emotions*. Empathy continues to be a premium in companies. Managers, especially, should build their empathy muscles, as they tend to set the tone for others in the workplace. Employees should feel heard or seen by their managers, and this requires empathy.

It takes deliberate thought and action to be able to imagine, even remotely, what life is like for someone else. It's the evolved version of "putting yourself in someone else's shoes." Over the years, I've begun to think of empathy as a core value that employees should strive for and exercise. It's important for others to be able to see beyond themselves, especially when we think about what it means to build teamwork.

To recap: we've outlined the following as commonplace feelings and emotional states that we would like to engage in at work:

Happiness
Trust
Vulnerability
Compassion
Empathy

PAUSE AND PONDER

On a scale of 1–5, with one being "Least Likely" and 5 being "Very Likely," rate how likely you are to feel these emotions in your current work environment:

1. How likely are you to experience feelings of happiness at work?
2. How likely are you to feel that you can trust your manager?
3. How likely are you to feel that you can trust your teammates?
4. How likely are you to feel that you can be vulnerable at work?
5. How likely are you to experience feelings of compassion at work?
6. How likely are you to experience feelings of empathy at work?

"Per My Last Email" Feelings

Now onto feelings that are very normal but aren't ones we'd like to engage in frequently because they don't make us feel good and will likely impact or influence others. For those unfamiliar, "per my last email" has taken on a life of its own as the professionally acceptable way to express passive aggression or even just aggression with coworkers.

Anger   A feeling that occurs when something gets in the way of the desired outcome or when we believe there's a violation of the way things should be. It's often a burst of intense feeling. Anger tends to foster action because as humans, we want to do something with it. Research has shown that anger tends to be an immediate feeling that usually entails a secondary emotion. Essentially, anger is not just anger alone. Behind it could be emotions like fear, anxiety, rejection, frustration, or hurt with the goal of resolution. We know that if we hold on to anger, it eventually festers into other effects of emotional exhaustion, such as resentment. Anger is an easy emotion to access. I have walked away from meetings angry and unsure of how to manage my feelings. I recall during a debrief about potential candidates for open roles that as we scored candidates by our internal criteria, one of the senior leaders seemed to be evaluating by a different set of qualifications. I was frustrated, and instead of acknowledging the miscommunication, my responses were short and unproductive. We didn't find an immediate resolution and were unable to move forward in determining next steps.

Frustration   Frustration occurs when actions or impulses prevent an expected outcome. As in, you expected a certain outcome and it didn't happen. Frustration in the workplace can stem from many different sources, from poor communication to office bureaucracy to unproductive management.

Disappointment   Disappointment is a feeling resulting from unmet expectations. We've all experienced disappointment at one point or another. Jasmine recalls a handful of times when she felt disappointed over promised promotions that didn't happen: "It's like you can be a rockstar, but there is no promotion to give if the position is not there for you. That's when I learned that sometimes promotions aren't about merit. Sometimes, it's just good luck and timing."

I genuinely hate feeling disappointed—both in myself and in others. It reminds me of that mom joke: "I'm not mad, I'm disappointed." Which just makes you feel worse? Personally, I'm all for feeling anger; disappointment is one beast of an emotion I try to avoid.

Envy   Envy is often mistaken for jealousy. But envy refers to the desire for what someone else has. In contrast, jealousy refers to already owning something (generally, a relationship) and having it threatened. A good example of envy is when people say, "I'm jealous that they got promoted," but they really mean to say, "I'm envious of their promotion." In the workplace, envy usually comes in the form of expressing insecurity. I've found myself envious of certain coworkers for the praise they received. It wasn't that it wasn't warranted (it was!), it was more of "I wish I could've done the thing they did." Envy doesn't have to be malicious. It's often more of a reflection of ourselves and our desires. As I write this, I think about all the times I've probably been envious of someone's promotion—not because I didn't think they deserved it, but mostly because I wanted the acknowledgment for myself.

Stress or Overwhelm   Like envy and jealousy, stress and overwhelm are often used interchangeably, but the difference is in intensity levels and how they impact our ability to function. Stress results when we can't successfully cope with our environments. Feeling overwhelmed means experiencing an extreme level of stress or cognitive intensity to the point of not being able to function.

I cry quickly, but I release a particular type of cry that indicates to me that I am overwhelmed. It's the cry that finally listens to my body. This cry tightens the muscles in my body and has been slowly building. You know the cry. I hate when

I let myself get to that point because it means I'm probably burning out. I used to work at an emerging beverage brand called Golden, and as a project manager, my role required that I worked with several different teams, which meant a lot of work. I was so constantly overwhelmed when I looked at my to-do list that I would just sit in paralysis, wondering how I would ever get it done.

Reframing Positive and Negative Emotions

In a recent interview on the podcast *Unlocking Us with Brené Brown*, author and NFL football player, Emmanuel Acho, stated that one of the most dangerous things to lead with is the saying, "Well, it's always been done that way." His revelation struck a chord with me. As someone who often doesn't mind playing by the rules, the reality is that it doesn't have to always be "that way." In Chapter 1, we examined how societal norms impact the way that we exist in the office. The office is a microcosm of the different dynamics at play in our society—gender, race, and socioeconomic status—that have all culminated into the similar framing that positive emotions are good and negative emotions are bad.

This way of thinking fails to take into consideration that feelings, good or bad, happen on a spectrum. We can feel good things for a short period and also feel not-so-good things later. When we box the idea of emotions into simply "positive" or "negative," we're limiting the language available to describe how we feel. As managers, if we simply default to these descriptors, we are often left with unconstructive feedback for our direct reports.

Good versus bad is a binary and linear approach to understanding why we feel the things we feel. Emotions are normal and healthy. Being angry or disappointed isn't a bad thing. On the contrary, constant positive emotions aren't realistic. Let's be honest, we all secretly despise that one chipper morning person (if that's me, sorry!) at the office or the coffee shop. Positive emotions don't necessarily equate to positive outcomes and vice versa. Often, life's hardest and most challenging moments generate lifelong learnings.

In the spirit of challenging "the way" or the status quo, I pushed myself to reframe what it means to have positive or negative emotions. I wondered about the implications of having a binary view of emotions and found myself thinking more specifically about the actions that come right after these feelings. I wondered about the intended output—how do we want to feel afterward? What are we hoping for from our colleagues when we express our feelings of frustration or compassion? Every work environment elicits a wide range of great feelings and not-so-great feelings for its employees. Like life, we can't predict how things will turn out or how projects will go, but can we at least start creating a path to what these feelings mean to us and how we manage them?

Zooming out, we tend to think about positive emotions as markers of flourishing or optimal well-being. We associate them with past experiences or memories that evoke feelings such as joy, happiness, and pride. To further our understanding of the impact of positive emotions and how they can transform our lives, psychology professor Dr. Barbara Fredrickson created the "broaden-and-build theory of positive emotions." This theory describes the formation of positive emotions in terms of building enduring personal resources. Fredrickson provides evidence that suggests that experiencing positive emotions broadens the scopes of attention, cognition, and action and that they build physical, intellectual, and social resources. In short, as humans, when we lean into positive emotions and thoughts, such as play or joy, we inevitably develop actions that will use physical and mental resources. In contrast, negative emotions tend to narrow our attention, limiting our scopes of cognition and action. In layman's terms, positive emotions can inspire action, whereas negative emotions may inspire inaction.

Positive emotions = inspired emotions
Negative emotions = uninspired emotions

Merriam-Webster defines "inspire" as "to move or guide by divine influence." If we can start to frame "inspired emotions" such as happiness, trust, compassion, and empathy as eliciting behavior, I believe we can encourage inspired actions that propel productive progression.

My goal with using vocabulary such as "inspire" is to create a sense of warmth and benevolence in the workplace. While I don't believe semantics can change the essence of work situations, I do believe semantics play a role in crafting and shifting perspective. And, in this case, I wonder how using "inspired" can provide a mini-action step in between someone expressing a feeling and someone receiving it. I'd like to think that this framing can add a bit of cushion to how we share feelings.

In a similar vein, I like taking the idea of "uninspired" and applying it to those emotions—such as anger, disappointment, envy, and stress—that tend to make people feel exhausted or unmotivated. The idea here is that sharing uninspiring emotions doesn't create a "stop" in motion; it opens an opportunity to inject support or a sense of security back into a situation. We often express feelings of anger or frustration when we feel something is disrupting the thing we're trying to achieve—usually this comes in the form of receiving feedback (solicited or unsolicited) or hearing things that may deflect a point we're making.

Tapping into more of a cognitive way of looking at feelings, Adlerian theory, or individual therapy, is a goal-oriented and generally positive psychodynamic therapy. A student of Sigmund Freud, Alfred Adler developed his theory with a holistic approach, emphasizing the importance of overcoming feelings of inferiority and gaining a sense of belonging to achieve happiness and fulfilling social connections. In a nutshell, Adler theorizes that we as humans all have the goal of self-fulfillment and self-actualization. He argues that depressed people tend to have low impressions of themselves, caused by the belief that they had the opportunity to do something or get something they believed was truly valuable. Adler describes the individual as becoming discouraged when this opportunity is not achieved. While I disagree that depression is a side effect of being discouraged, I resonated with the idea that we can feel demotivated and discouraged when we are not able to meet our goals. My hope is that adding this mini action step of defining emotions as inspired or uninspired creates a bit more nuance in the way that we perceive feeling emotions at work.

TOO LONG; DIDN'T READ

This is going to sound corny, but having awareness of your emotions is powerful. Like all things in life, words matter, and having a core baseline of emotions, or in this case, an emotion directory will help generate collective emotional fluency, leaving your team clear language to use when describing how they feel. The goal is to close the gap between the dissonance of feelings and words. It's a muscle that requires practice and consistency or else it loses its strength. While we can't always identify these feelings in others, our goal should be to use this language to spark healthy and meaningful conversations about how we're feeling.

PAUSE AND PONDER

- What emotions or feelings would you incorporate in your own emotion directory?
- What are some everyday work situations in which describing your feelings would be helpful? Employee engagement surveys? 360 peer feedback?

Internal Communications Policy

As we examined in Chapter 1, work culture is influenced by gender, racial, and socioeconomic norms. We also explored why creating space for employees is critical to their experience. Work culture brings together cognitive and emotional values. Cognitive values refer to how we get work done, think efficiency and performance, whereas emotional values outline how employees should feel and emote in the workspace.

We've covered how workplace culture came to be, but now we'll get into how we begin to speak and build the emotional language we'll need to develop or shift our emotional work culture. Using the same ideas of inspired or uninspired feelings, we'll be looking at company cultures as either inspired or uninspired. Let's explore the defining characteristics for both of these emotional cultures.

Defining an Inspired Emotional Work Culture

What do you think about when you think of a positive work culture? Does the company have amazing perks? Are you able to speak up on topics you agree or don't agree with? Is it a place where marginalized employees can feel safe openly sharing their thoughts or feelings? When I think about my career thus far, I can count the number of positive work environments I've been in on one hand. When I asked Elizabeth about the culture at her current company, an HR management solution focused on employee engagement, she shared:

My company showed me it was a positive work culture immediately. When I started remotely in March 2020, people went out of their way to make me feel included. This included putting time on my calendar to meet and learn about me, which is standard practice to this day.

After only six weeks, when I was laid off, they gave me three months of severance, paid me in one cash lump sum for COBRA through 2020, and let me keep my laptop. Even in tough times, they treated me well. After the layoff, I sent an email to my chief customer officer, thanking her for the opportunity and for showing me what I'm looking for in a company moving forward. She responded that the email made her tear up and genuinely hoped I'd consider the company again in the future. When I came back three months later, the company was so excited. I got outreach from almost the whole C suite (individually and privately) welcoming me back. During my first all-hands back, the Zoom chat lit up with people sharing love and excitement that I was back.

A few months later, I had a customer with whom I just didn't vibe. The situation got tense, he was very disrespectful, and I told my manager I felt emotionally unsafe around this customer. Nothing else was said. He reached out to the customer and reassigned the account. It wasn't a battle for me to fight. My manager wanted to protect me before anything else.

The concept of positivity isn't bursts of sunshine and rainbows. We shouldn't lean into an overexaggeration of positive behaviors; rather, we should explore together what we can do to cultivate progressive feelings and actions. We should be striving for what Wharton management professor Sigal Barsade calls "compassionate love." Compassionate love, in this case when coworkers are considerate and care about each other, is vital to team morale and environments. Within a more inspiring work culture, we should also anticipate that feelings will exist on a spectrum and the work environment needs to be inclusive in terms of both the anxiety and the joy that comes with being a human at work. "When colleagues who are together day in and day out ask and care about each other's work and even nonwork issues," Barsade says, "they are careful of each other's feelings. They show compassion when things don't go well. And they also show affection and caring—and that can be about bringing somebody a cup of coffee when you go get your own, or just listening when a coworker needs to talk."

Barsade and her team conducted several studies that measured tenderness, compassion, affection, and caring. But rather than simply asking the participants if they felt or expressed those emotions themselves, the researchers asked to what degree people saw their colleagues expressing them. One of the most critical findings in the study was that a compassionate work culture led to higher levels of employee engagement and lower levels of employee burnout and absenteeism. An inspired work culture does not mean that it's devoid of conflict. Instead, the idea of a compassionate culture is to be accepting of all authentic emotions such as sadness, fear, or disappointment, and to work together in finding solutions (or rather a state of emotional equilibrium).

As Elizabeth shared, her company *showed* her what kind of company they were, reinforced by acts of compassion (giving her fair severance and following up with an opportunity) and explicitly verbalizing how they personally care (colleagues and leadership reaching out to share how thrilled they were she came back on). These characteristics are what transform employees' experiences from good to great. Let's focus on a few key elements that help shape an inspired working culture.

Care Personally and Empathize

In *Radical Candor: Be a Kick-Ass Boss Without Losing Your Humanity*, author Kim Scott encourages managers to care personally about the people who report to them and let them know when they aren't in alignment. She writes: "Caring personally is the antidote to both robotic professionalism and managerial arrogance." The act of caring requires multiple feelings, such as compassion and empathy.

A recent study examined a group of English-speaking individuals and found that negative attitudes toward non-English-speaking individuals decreased once participants received perspective-taking training (otherwise known as developing empathy). By completing a recipe in silence, imagining that they could not speak or understand English, and using instructions in an abstract, non-English language, the participants experienced how non-English-speaking individuals work in the kitchen. The change in attitudes suggests that the participants were less likely to view non-English-speaking individuals as outsiders when they acted with empathy.

Elizabeth experienced this type of compassion when her manager listened and transferred her tough client to another person. The manager illustrated that they cared by actively listening to Elizabeth and then following up with a course of action. We should care about each other's humanity. As obvious as it sounds, it's not an obvious virtue for many companies.

Create a Sense of Belongingness

According to research conducted by BetterUp—a mobile-based platform focused on coaching, mentoring, and counseling—and the *Harvard Business Review*, if workers feel like they belong, companies gain substantial bottom-line benefits. Studies show that "high belonging was linked to a whopping 56% increase in job performance, a 50% drop in turnover risk, and a 75% reduction in sick days."

If you've ever seen the diagram of Maslow's hierarchy of needs, you know that social belonging is a fundamental human necessity. In *No Hard Feelings: The Secret Power of Embracing Emotions at Work*, Liz Fosslien and Mollie West Duffy describe belonging as a sense of safety and feeling valued for embracing what makes you different. For Elizabeth, belongingness came in the form of being personally welcomed back by the executive team and then publicly welcomed back by the entire organization. Despite her being laid off, both the organization and Elizabeth welcomed each other back with open arms.

Work with Integrity

Integrity is the sauce that makes people believe and trust you. The formal definition of integrity refers to characteristics and work ethic that include respect, reliability, sound judgment, and openness. In many workplaces, integrity acts as a moral compass: it's better to do the right thing than to be right.

Elizabeth's manager exhibited integrity by listening to her concerns regarding her client and taking immediate action to course correct. It would've been easier for Elizabeth's manager to placate her in the interim or dismiss her concerns to avoid the risk of client conflict, but by supporting Elizabeth, her manager demonstrated integrity by keeping his word while also exhibiting sound judgment and openness.

Avoid Blame and Encourage Forgiving Mistakes

Blame can be described as exhibiting destructive behaviors such as criticism, contempt, defensiveness, and stonewalling. Blame is naturally wired into us; we tend to blame others or circumstances when things go wrong even when we know that mistakes happen from time to time.

It was probably very easy to blame the company for the layoffs in Elizabeth's case. I'm guilty of blaming previous employers for crappy circumstances and not having the greatest attitude about it. However, Elizabeth's company seemed genuinely invested in her development despite the unfortunate financial circumstances that caused her layoff. For the record, laying people off is emotionally taxing and hard. I can't imagine what Elizabeth's manager must've felt, considering Elizabeth was a recent hire. Still, Elizabeth's experience was positive overall, which inevitably led her back to the company.

Emphasize the Meaningfulness of the Work

Work meaningfulness is the perception of personal significance and value that we attach to work. When employees have a high sense of meaning in work, they are more likely to be motivated to complete their work. This type of meaningful work satisfies our high-level needs of belonging, esteem, and self-actualization in Maslow's hierarchy of needs. To be clear, there is not one way to create meaning at work. For some, it may be simple acknowledgment or affirmation from a manager, and, for others, it might be being part of a team that you love. Statistics indicate that the level of effort and care that Elizabeth's company has shown her will likely motivate her to stay at the company—she finds value in her work and feels valuable to the organization because of the company's actions.

TOO LONG; DIDN'T READ

Quick review: an inspired work culture should include some of the following characteristics:

- Deep care and empathy
- A sense of belonging
- Absence of blame and encouragement of forgiving mistakes
- Emphasis on the meaningfulness of the work

These are just a few characteristics that enable an inspired work culture. What others come to mind?

It's important to note that the salience of an inspired work culture does have its limitations. There has not been sufficient research to illustrate if there are boundary conditions across different segments of employees. Understanding the various cultural contexts can anticipate where and when tension may exist within the work environment. But again, an inspired work culture should also include uninspired feelings because they're wired into us. As managers, we should think about reacting to such emotions productively. We should note how and which inspired emotions are displayed and how we can create policies that help cement these ideas. We will touch more on tangible ways to show how we can implement emotional shifts later on.

___| PAUSE AND PONDER |_____

–   Are there other characteristics that you've found that help contribute to an inspiring work culture?
–   Of the characteristics listed above, were there any you were surprised by? Were there any that you have not experienced (yet)?

Defining an Uninspired Emotional Work Culture

When she worked at an agency and had a dismissive manager, Jasmine recalled,

> I had a very judgmental manager [who was] not understanding. Which meant I kept a lot of my feelings to myself. It broke me down. I was stressed out planning my wedding—flying back from Atlanta to New York. There was a lot of stuff at work as well. I couldn't share any of this with my manager because I knew she wouldn't be accommodating or understanding. I just knew I couldn't trust my feelings. Sometimes I would go to a different floor and just cry in the bathroom. Wipe my tears, wipe my face. And go back to work. It was not an environment that was

understanding—you had to pretend that everything was fine and you just pushed through. If anything, it was a testament that it wasn't a great place. As soon as I hit my one-year mark, I left. That's when I really learned that culture was important. I ended up taking a lateral move to another company, and it's been one of the best work experiences I've had in my life.

Experiences like Jasmine's are unfortunately common. Harboring negative feelings, especially emotions such as sadness or anger, makes it increasingly difficult to be pro- ductive. According to a study, employees who have negative experiences tend to lose motivation and project their negative feelings onto others. They also find ways to avoid coworkers and circumstances that they associate with their negative feelings, which can impact communication and resourcing. The suppression of emotions, whether positive or negative, affects an employee's self-monitoring and self-regulation processes, taxing the individual's cognitive and emotional resources. Simply put, it's emotionally and physically draining to hold all of these emotions.

There are enormous consequences of negative work culture. It reinforces harmful norms such as suppression being a mode of self-preservation. Employees may suppress their feelings to maintain the status quo or withdraw from an inter- action. Suppression cements the idea that employees cannot look at work as a psychologically safe space. Bradley reflected on a time at his former advertising agency when a senior-level executive publicly scolded him.

I've had some real asshole bosses. There was a time when I was working at an agency, and I recall making a mistake. To have this grown, 47-year-old white woman looking over my shoulder and yelling at me. Having moments like that was pretty demean- ing. I felt worthless and felt like I was not in a place to respond because a white woman was stern and yelling at a Black man. Okay. A Black man yelling and being stern with a white woman

*(who is also his superior, let's not lose sight of that) wouldn't even
be okay. I think because I'm a Black man, specifically, I'm not
allowed to respond the same way they're talking to me.*

Moments like the above can induce feelings of rage. It
emphasizes how debilitating it can be to not be able to stand
up for yourself or, in some cases, have others stand up for you,
out of fear. A landmark study published in 2001 shows that the
brain responds more strongly to bad experiences than good
ones and our memories retain them longer. It's like when we
tend to recall the worst parts of a relationship first during a
breakup. We react and remember those parts more.

Low Team Morale and Energy

Team morale is defined as how employees feel about their
work. Positive morale is generally seen as the fuel behind team
motivation, while negative morale contributes to absenteeism,
poor performance, and employee discontent. Companies that
fail to address low morale issues could face decreased productivity, increased rates of absenteeism and associated costs,
increased conflicts in the work environment, and increased
employee turnover rates.

I once worked at a creative agency where we were working
down to the wire on every project deadline. I can't recall if
anybody was ever in a good mood. I do recall a freelancer
candidly sharing that "everyone seemed miserable," and I didn't
disagree. Sometimes you just know there's a bad vibe where
no one seems excited for or motivated by the work. If you start
hearing that people are dreading the work environment, it might
be wise to investigate why.

Lack of Psychological Safety to Speak Up

Psychological safety is the ability for an individual to be candid
in the workplace. In a psychologically safe environment,

interpersonal risks, like speaking up with questions, concerns, ideas, and even mistakes, feels doable. The opposite of psychological safety can look like many different things, such as a manager silencing a direct report, no new ideas ever suggested by the team, and employees being afraid of making a mistake. Research has found that in the absence of psychological safety, people hide their mistakes in order to protect themselves. When errors aren't detected, they get repeated, thus increasing potential risk and harm.

In some cases, lack of psychological safety has resulted in the loss of dollars. My team was on a call with a partner agency that was on the hook for creating videos for us to use in an upcoming marketing campaign for Mansion. After reviewing the storyboards, we felt pretty strongly that the agency missed the mark on our creative brief. However, our CEO didn't think so. Truthfully, her response felt like dissent and punishment. It wasn't that our CEO wasn't approachable. Her creative pedigree often dictated the direction of our creative pursuits. A few of us felt like we couldn't necessarily voice opposition because some had already been either rejected or reprimanded by her previously. In essence, we didn't feel safe opposing her.

Considering those previous experiences, no one objected to the storyboards despite not feeling confident in the preproduction work. Well, the result was crap. It was usable, but we felt like we had wasted a ton of money for subpar content. As much as I wanted to be a hater and blame the vendor, it wasn't completely their fault. After all, they did receive approval from our CEO. If we had felt psychologically safe to voice our true feelings, perhaps the outcome would have been different.

Lack of Trust Between Teammates or Leadership

Trust is fundamentally essential for any team. "Trust is the foundation of every relationship in our life," says Jen Fisher, Chief Well-Being Officer for the U.S. at the consultancy firm Deloitte.

"Every positive relationship starts from a place of trust." When trust is violated, we can see it manifest in a few ways:

- Silence despite disagreement
- Concerted effort to avoid spending time together, which leads to poor productivity
- Information not being properly distributed
- Circumventing someone by going to a manager or other teammates
- Venting sessions that can transform into office gossip
- Micromanagement

Gallup research reveals that companies with high trust levels outperform those with low trust levels by 186%. Trust can be damaged in two directions: between employees and leadership, and between employees.

Trust Between Employees and Leadership

When employees lack trust in their leadership, they tend to be at a higher risk of leaving the company. Employees tend to be disengaged and dissatisfied with work especially if promises are broken by leadership. This lack of trust also develops its own sense of trickle-down trust issues, meaning it continues to spread.

Trust Between Employees

If teammates don't trust each other, there can be serious consequences such as holding onto key information, blocking productivity, and eventually blocking the organization from moving forward.

I worked at an early-stage startup consisting of four part-time freelancers across marketing and design. Like any scrappy startup, it was all hands on deck all the time. The creative director was the main photographer for all our creative shoots in the early days. To streamline smaller creative projects, our design lead and head of marketing outsourced a photographer for a small partnership project. In our minds, the project was low-risk, considering the image would only be shared on the partner's Instagram page. The photographer we enlisted was local, could provide content quickly, and was also able to capture film. The result was mediocre at best, but, again, it was low-risk so most of us found it rather acceptable given its priority. All of us except our creative director that is, who voiced massive concern over the images and demanded that she reshoot the entire thing.

Our design lead collaborated with our head of marketing on a solution to save cost and time. Understanding that it would only be one to two photos that would live on our partner's page, our design lead quickly edited a few photos that fell nicely within our art direction and general design guidelines. The email was written with care to our founder and was shared as a reasonable solution to our predicament. Our creative director responded: "With all due respect, I own the company, and I disagree."

I've worked at many places with different types of personalities, but there are a few things that are permanently etched in my mind, and that response is one of them. (As you might recall from the last section, we tend to remember bad experiences more than we do good ones.) From that point on, it felt like any creative idea or execution from our design lead was made with hesitation in an attempt to avoid the possibility of re-experiencing that moment. You can imagine that lack of trust in our leadership led to poor productivity and created a ton of unnecessary barriers to movement, especially in design. As the operations person, it was a pain in the ass to navigate as a mediator between the design team and to see first-hand how unproductive and unhelpful it was for the organization.

Shitty Leadership

I once worked for a company where it seemed like everyone strongly disliked the CEO. (I would later find out it was for good reason.) He was smart and witty, but very clearly, he was an asshole. I distinctly remember that he called a certain section of the office the "hen house" during our in-person onboarding because mostly women sat there. He seemed emotionally uneven most of the time and was known for random outbursts of anger. Yet, everyone else in the office seemed to let him throw tantrums and excuse his shitty behavior.

Fortunately, he was in Los Angeles and I was part of the New York office, but it pained me whenever we learned that he would be visiting our office. While the rest of the leadership team was thoughtful and intelligent, he always bulldozed over them in meetings. Issues with the product started emerging, but somehow, he always had an explanation or plan to cover the company's missteps.

Suffice it to say, I was not a fan. After three months, I quit, simply stating that if I had to imagine myself here for the next six to twelve months, I would be unsatisfied, and it would be best to bring on someone else who would appreciate the opportunity more than me.

When dealing with shitty leadership, look to other executive management team members to become the embodiment of cultural values. Remember that sometimes that founder isn't the end-all-be-all of a company.

According to a 2013 meta-analysis of 57 different studies published in the *Leadership Quarterly*, there is a very high correlation between destructive leadership and negative attitudes toward the leader. Surprisingly, the next highest correlation was found between destructive leadership and counterproductive work behavior. In layman's terms: if your CEO sucks, you'll not only start disliking them but you'll probably start acting like them. We'll talk more about emotional contagion later, but effectively this means that shitty behavior you dislike in your boss will likely be replicated by you and your teammates toward each other. Fun.

To recap, some key characteristics of uninspired work culture are:

- Low team morale and energy
- Lack of psychological safety to speak up
- Lack of trust between teammates or leadership
- Shitty leadership

It's important to recognize if these characteristics exist within your own work culture. Not only does it impact the team, but it inevitably impacts the company's bottom line. We'll get into more detail about how this impacts company dollars in the long run later.

__| PAUSE AND PONDER |_____

- What are the characteristics and elements that made a work environment inspired or uninspired for you?
- Did you have a prominent role in helping define your work culture?
- Reflect on a previous work environment. Was that culture explicitly told to you? Or was it implied?

Employee Code of Conduct

How you gon' win when you ain't right within?
—Lauryn Hill

Leaning into Lauryn Hill's classic bop, "Doo Wop (That Thing)," we've done a lot of exploration of the distinct characteristics of work culture. In that time, we've also woven in some self-assessment around how we process emotions and how they are expressed in the workplace. Let's start piecing all of these things together. Ready?

Arlie Hochschild, an American sociologist and academic who has done critically acclaimed studies on workers' and caregivers' emotional lives, introduced the concept of "feeling rules." Feeling rules are social norms that outline how people should feel in particular situations, providing guidelines for labeling, assessing, managing, and expressing our emotions. Hochschild argues that people actively manipulate their emotions to match feeling rules. She labels the process as "emotion management" or the work required to induce or inhibit feelings by rendering them "appropriate" to a situation. If the feeling rules feel (pun intended) familiar, they should: this is how we also describe emotional values when we outline work culture.

Let's also remember how these feeling rules are inherently informed by macrosystems such as race, gender, and socioeconomic status, and how they've helped us develop those internal scripts, an implicit set of feeling rules that are the workplace or cultural norm, regarding how we should emote and act at work. As part of these internal scripts, we tend to carry out emotional labor. Also coined by Hochschild, "emotional labor" is the work of managing personal feelings in a professional context, particularly in public-facing jobs where employees work to produce a particular emotional effect among their peers. Think back to Chapter 1, where we talked about surface and deep acting. "Surface acting" is centered around faking emotions for work's sake, whereas "deep acting" focuses on putting effort into actually feeling and expressing the true emotions. As part of emotional labor, we tend to fall into either of these forms of expression depending on the script we need to carry out. For many non-white and Black people, we often hear that we perform emotional labor to survive predominantly white environments. Sean recalled,

I was employee number seven at my last job and the only Black person there. But as the company continued to grow, the same

variation of people kept getting hired: white. It created an internal conflict, like, why am I here among this group? It was clear who the brand identified and targeted and who they were recruiting (again, white women). It was compounded when my manager left; it felt like me fending for myself and reconciling how I fit in.

What are some familiar internal scripts that would induce emotional labor and require employees to rely on surface acting?

When an Employee Responds to Critical Feedback   Recall Bradley's story of being reprimanded publicly by his white female supervisor.

When an Employee Feels Overwhelmed   Jasmine frequented a different floor's bathroom whenever she felt the need to cry because of the lack of emotional support at her workplace. Despite feeling overwhelmed, she put on a "strong" face to appear unaffected.

When Employees Lack Trust in Their Manager   With the lack of psychological safety, my team did not feel comfortable sharing productive feedback with our manager and our previous experiences. We metaphorically faked smiles.

The reality is that we see these types of scripts play out all around us every day. We've been both the person on the receiving end and the person who is potentially contributing to uninspired feelings. We have an opportunity to start challenging and redefining what those feeling rules can look like. How can we tap into a work culture that allows for more deep acting rather than surface acting? How can we enable healthier ways to express emotion in the hopes of creating space for others to join? As you develop your own feeling rules for your team, remember that each person uniquely processes experiences. Some may adjust quickly, and others might be highly hesitant for personal and professional reasons.

When we use the term "employee conduct," we're signing on to a company's rules on how we can and cannot behave during work hours. All organizations have codified values and rules that highlight exemplary employee conduct. They're usually laden with legal terms. But in our case, let's flip the idea of a code of conduct on its head and outline how we can develop conduct based on what we've learned so far. In the following sections, I will outline seven guiding principles:

1. Develop cultural humility
2. Model inspiring behavior
3. Emote (or don't emote) contagious behavior
4. Address negative emotions on the onset
5. Be accountable, not performative
6. Craft psychological safety
7. Develop policy to anticipate emotional needs
8. Lean into ambiguity with curiosity

These principles can help influence how you can approach building team culture one action at a time. Lauryn said it—we have to be right within ourselves if we want to win.

Develop Cultural Humility

"I should have been promoted for not beating his ass," reflected Kwanza as he told me about a time when a former head of a department scolded him. The head of the department in question had received a complaint that Kwanza was posting anonymously on the internet. At the time, blogging was just emerging; we're talking before Facebook, before all of that. Although the post did not mention anything related to the workplace, a colleague decided it was inappropriate and wanted him to get reprimanded.

The department head told Kwanza: "What we do in private can sometimes be a reflection of the company. How would you feel if you knew I was burning crosses in my yard this weekend?"

His response left Kwanza astonished. How did an anonymous blog post compare to racist acts of violence? Would the same department head use the same example if Kwanza were white? Why did he feel that was appropriate? (For what it's worth, years later, the same department head appeared at a Halloween party with a suspicious robe that was not made to look like a wizard. I'll just leave that there.) How could the head of the department better handle the complaint against Kwanza? An obvious way of avoiding friction is probably not to mention violence in any context in the workplace. Kwanza's head of department clearly lacked cultural humility (and common sense).

Developing cultural humility is part of developing cultural competence. By virtue of existing in a multicultural society, cultural competence is integral to one's code of ethics.

For example, the American Counseling Association's code of ethics states that for counselors to be culturally competent, individuals must be open-minded and value and respect cultural differences. This level of awareness requires a commitment to lifelong learning and making sound ethical decisions within diverse cultural contexts. Let's break down the term to fully understand its roots. "Competence" is the ability to do something efficiently or successfully. "Cultural" refers to the ideas, behaviors, or customs related to a society. Therefore, cultural competence is the ability to understand and respect values, attitudes, and beliefs in relation to another person. Cultural humility can be seen as two-pronged: it means admitting that we don't know everything and are willing to learn from others about their experiences while being aware of our own biases, values, and place in society.

In other words, as a Filipino woman I can learn all about Ramadan but that knowledge will not apply to me unless I can contextualize that information within a relationship. If my best friend is Muslim, I am more likely to know about Ramadan in context of their life and can continue to learn more about the culture through this relationship. Cultural competence suggests *mastery*, while humility is about cultivating self-awareness through introspection and refers to an awareness of the perspective of others. As Dr. Gideon Litherland, clinical lecturer and clinical training director in the counseling program at the Family Institute at Northwestern University, notes, "You can't have competence without humility."

Given these definitions, what does it mean to have cultural humility at work? Most companies' diversity and inclusion teams put forth strategies to develop humility—think equitable and diverse hiring practices or implicit bias training. These tactics are all geared toward building competency and affirming diversity.

One popular approach to achieving multicultural harmony in the workplace is diversity training. A recent survey found that up to 79% of organizations used some form of diversity training. Here are some examples of cultural humility in the workplace:

- Highlighting and emphasizing saying peoples' names correctly and addressing individuals by their correct pronouns.
- Developing employee resource groups (ERGs) to create a platform for employees and, more importantly, to foster community and camaraderie.
- Gathering data from employees about their views on culture; the goal being to derive learnings that can help inform policies or programming that increases cultural sensitivity and awareness.

The reason that I emphasize humility versus competence in this book is that cultural competency tends to end at cultural discourse. While that is important and the ultimate goal, I think it's a safe bet that a lot of us fall into the bucket of needing to build humility first. As mentioned, humility is a process-oriented approach, and process requires action. In addition to being willing to learn about others' culture, we must also be able to examine our own biases, values, and culture through introspection. Think about how you show up for others: What parts of your identity are visible and not so visible?

In Kim Scott's *Just Work*, she reflects on her feedback from writing *Radical Candor*. While the book was a commercial success, Scott inevitably left out a huge aspect of radical candor: it didn't apply to everyone—just mostly white professionals. As a learning opportunity, Scott looked inward first to understand the development of this blind spot given her expertise in the field of organizational behavior. She noted her compounding privileges, as a white, nondisabled, cisgender, heterosexual, white woman. How have these privileges enabled her to develop the ability to be candid? What privileges was she afforded simply for existing? This is not meant to take away the impact of the radical candor approach, but rather adds a nuanced cultural element. By looking inward and being open to learning about the nuances, Scott has developed a more robust version of radical candor that notes the caveats in the process.

It's rather normal to have biases—you're human after all. If you knew how to check all your biases at the door, you'd hold one of life's deepest secrets. We're conditioned by the biases that we have and what we're taught. There is no such thing as being completely judgment free. We're not wired that way. But we can sit with our feelings of judgment and aim to understand why and where they come from. Key questions you can ask yourself:

- Am I feeling defensive about this judgment?
- Where do I think this idea or concept comes from? Childhood? Recent developments?
- Is this reinforcing a stereotype that I've been conditioned to believe is true?
- What does it mean to unlearn this thought?

Understanding and learning about how and why you function the way you do will help illuminate your path to cultural competency. Remember, these are all things that we've been conditioned to learn and that means that we can unlearn them.

Practicing cultural humility is a lot like treating others the way you want to be treated. Reciprocity is the guiding principle. The idea is that gaining perspective on someone else's cultural experience elicits empathy. When practicing cultural humility, you can always default to the adage: "If you don't know, then ask."

Developing cultural humility isn't a one-and-done process. Rather, it requires commitment and adaptability because our society is fragmented and nuanced. We evolve our norms through time. Things move even more quickly in the age of social media, and what was acceptable two years ago may not be acceptable now. This is a good thing. Again, humility is admitting what we don't know in order to learn more about each other. In the context of work, developing this skill set will enable teammates to better understand each other through empathy and openness, which will lead to more trust and chemistry and overall better team dynamics.

Model Inspiring Behavior

In Cognitive Behavioral Theory, a core aspect of treatment is developing compensatory strategies to cope with challenging situations. One method is called "modeling," which is when learning occurs through observation and imitation alone, without comment or reinforcement. Children are great at modeling. Think about toddlers and how they absorb and replicate actions they see you doing as a way to learn how to respond to their environment. Cassandra, a senior manager who works at an international education nonprofit organization, shares the influence of modeling on her management style.

I spent my first performance review just crying. I had a manager that had a personality that felt like you could be comfortable being emotional with her. She always checked in on me, which was the culture my manager showed me. I saw that and wanted to do the same thing for my team [of direct reports]. I would say that "being emotional" is not part of the department culture; I think it's something that certain people have as a value because of the managers who hired us. So, in this case, there are very few team leads [who] exhibit that similar type of openness and care with their teams.

What Cassandra experienced is a byproduct of affective events theory (AET), which centers on the connection between emotions and feelings in the workplace and its effect on job performance, job satisfaction, and behaviors.

You can use the AET framework to crystallize the four supporting ideas:

1. The nature, cause, and consequences of emotion in the workplace
2. The events cause emotional reactions in the workplace
3. The impact of emotion or attitude on job satisfaction
4. Emotional experiences tend to drive behavior and judgment

If the event is positive, there is likely to be a change if the employee experiences high job satisfaction with an assumption of strong work performance. The same logic would apply if the event were negative.

Positive work event/experience → positive emotions → (high) job satisfaction → positive work performance

Negative work event/experience → negative emotions → (low) job satisfaction → negative work performance

To zoom in, several of these relationships are more robust in the context of direct managers rather than organizational leaders. To that end, modeling behaviors are vital for managers and teams as they set an implicit standard for others. We tend to replicate what we see.

In her story, Cassandra had positive work experiences with her manager that influenced her as she developed her own management style. To boot, managers have a significant impact on the employee experience based on the AET framework. When you trust your manager, there's a higher chance that whatever they do rubs off on you one way or another.

Jasmine found herself in a complicated situation that did inevitably lead into a better work experience for herself and how she managed. She recalled:

> I remember when I had my hand slapped both times from my direct manager and my direct report. I had worked with this direct report for quite some time now and she was very much due for a promotion. She had shared with me that she didn't know if she could stay any longer and wanted to know when she could be promoted. The issue is that the company worked only within promotional periods. I recall telling her that she had delivered great work consistently and that she hadn't seen that great work translated into a promotion. However, if she felt like she couldn't wait any longer for that promotion cycle, I wouldn't hold it against her if she decided to move. I firmly believe that we should all take control of our careers and I wanted her to know that I was in support of that, having been there myself. I let my direct manager know about this conversation and I got reprimanded for encouraging her to look outside of the company. While I knew we prioritized retainment, it wasn't exactly spelled out to me. I was coming from the mindset that if we weren't able to give you what you want, then by all means get what you need. I got in trouble for that. Then my direct report got mad at me for telling my direct manager about it. She felt that the conversation was private despite it being about her career development and more specifically, a promotion.

It felt strange—I felt like I was doing the thing managers do, advocating for their direct reports. I ended up setting up a meeting with both and essentially apologized for sharing despite the good intention.

Part of being a manager is being able to admit when you mess up. I'm not a prideful person so it wasn't about ego. She appreciated me saying that and it truly was a humbling experience for me. What I learned from that experience was that I should've asked her if I could share this conversation with my manager. It's something I do more frequently now as I manage different teams—checking in and asking straightforwardly, no matter the intention. She did end up leaving about 6 months later, before the promotional cycle.

While it was a positive turned negative turned positive-ish moment, it's not like my manager gave me anything I could use to convince my direct report to stay. This is part of the corporate bullshit that we have to deal with. I've just erred on being open and honest but doing so carefully.

It's worth mentioning that it's not only the negative behaviors that employees replicate that could lead to low job satisfaction. Models can influence a halo effect for behavior that might be less compassionate. For example, suppose that in one office yelling is an acceptable way of speaking to a direct report. Chances are that when a direct report becomes a manager, they'll also use yelling to get their point across. So what do we do with this great responsibility, and how can we best leverage model behavior?

First off, when managers are selected, they need to have a well-developed sense of self. Ideally, this person has a good grip on their communication style and the way they navigate the business world. Apart from the interpersonal work an individual should do (more on this later!), managers should look at the broader employee journey, optimizing on moments that can make incremental but significant impact. Take, for example, one-on-ones. Managers should leverage their one-on-ones

as an opportunity to develop a healthy emotional connection with their direct reports. These meetings should not feel like a checklist but rather a dialogue around different topics including their current workload as well as their goals and hopes for the future. Make sure that you make it clear to direct reports that their one on-one time will be judgment-free.

It is important to create an environment of safety and openness by sharing stories that can help give context to both peoples' experiences. The one-on-one should be a sounding board for your report, guiding them through the distinction between gossiping and venting. Another way to look at model behavior is to give managers insight and data around how the employee and the team might be feeling. Emotions are data points that help guide us in more ways than we expect. Your reports look to you on how to assess that data, so it's important to model what the standards should be. Mirroring behavior sets the tone within teams and further lays the foundation on how we start to identify as company, culture-wise. We'll get more into this later on the role of managers.

Emote (or Don't Emote) Contagious Feelings

People tend to "catch" feelings easily. Simply put, both positive and negative emotions are contagious. Suppose one employee is in a sour mood. In that case, there's a likely chance that their annoyance or anger can easily spread to other teammates. There's the saying that "one bad apple spoils the whole bunch." Studies show that emotional contagion most often occurs at a significantly less conscious level. We're not always aware when someone else's mood impacts us.

Equally important when discussing emotional contagion is that not all expressions of feelings are verbal. Oftentimes, our body language and facial expressions are strong indicators of emotion. Think about what it means when you're speaking to someone and their arms are crossed. Or when you're sharing exciting news with a teammate and they seem unresponsive. Without saying much, some of these actions say a lot. This is a very silly example, but I am prone to copying repetitive physical actions. I had a manager who used to play with her hair during calls, and in a matter of a few weeks, I also was playing with my hair during calls.

So how do we counter spreading explicitly uninspired emotions? The reality is that some emotions are valid, but the idea is that they shouldn't stick around longer than necessary. Google originally coined the term "micro-moments" to refer to developing a marketing strategy that aligns with a customer's journey. Their thinking is that micro-moments occur when people reflexively turn to a device—increasingly a smart-phone—to act on a need to learn something, do something, discover something, watch something, or buy something. We should look at the idea of sharing daily "micro-moments" as a counteraction—think small, kind gestures versus big, bold declarations. Essentially taking that same idea of motivation and reflexively turning to a teammate with a positive gesture rather than a device.

Micro-moments reflect a sense of relatability that we desire as humans. Relatability comes in the form of those little experiences with others. In many ways, this takes the form of the proverbial water cooler talk. Academics and researchers Arlen Moller, Edward Deci, and Andrew Elliott discovered that each day an employee initiated a positive, relatable interaction with another person, that person became incrementally more positive in that environment. Additionally, the researchers found that more moments of kindness and general relatability led to higher goodwill toward the overall organization. Note that I use the terms "kindness" and "goodwill" versus happiness. Again, I want us to stay away from false platitudes and accept the reality that we can generally push forward small acts of kindness by simply having moments of relatability.

When we show a caring and compassionate mindset, studies have shown there is a higher record for modeling value-based positive behaviors. Again, this is where mirroring behaviors is integral to team health. The science shows that in a compassionate mindset, the givers' and receivers' brains release positive neurotransmitters that expand their ability to offer emotional transcendence. In other words, your brain recognizes that mindset and will likely replicate it because of the good feelings that it's generated. Think of these micro-moments as a way of A/B testing which initiatives or measures resonate well with your team. Researchers recommend starting off small—effortless acts or gestures such as creating a #Kudos channel on your internal messaging platform to give props to individuals or teams. Whatever action you decide on, it needs to feel real and genuine. There's nothing worse than when employees feel forced into engaging with each other or having to create false moments of togetherness.

Another way to encourage micro-moments is to use them as an opportunity to show praise. Bradley shares a tactic that he's been doing and encourages more of his colleagues to follow. He is one of a few men who work at a major women's skincare brand. Throughout his time there, he has observed that his teammates have glossed over suggestions or ideas from his other teammates, who are generally women. If Bradley shares the same idea, it seems to gain more attention. As a way to counter that behavior, Bradley developed his own micro-moment that whenever he seconded an idea, he would make sure to credit the original person. For example, "I love that idea that Yesenia shared earlier. I think it's a great way to engage our newer audiences." This is often referred to as "amplification." Interestingly enough, amplification was an approach that many Obama aides leveraged during his presidency to fight gender bias. When a woman made a key point, other women would repeat it, giving credit to its author. This forced the men in the room to recognize the contribution and denied them the chance to claim the idea as their own.

Other ways to counter negative emotional contagion include using humor. I used to start the day on Slack with a silly question in the hopes of inspiring laughter. I always felt that starting the day with a team laugh set the tone for the rest of the week and led to feelings of openness and joy permeating throughout the team, despite us being remote.

Emotional contagion is as sticky as it sounds. We look to each other as guiding lights as to how we feel at work. Countering negative emotional contagion requires awareness and a sense of responsibility from individuals. Like any sickness or disease, it requires time, patience, and a plan for recovery. This can come in the forms of micro-moments or humor. The idea here is to be able to catch the contagious emotion, especially if it falls into the uninspiring category, early enough before it becomes a problem. Similar to catching a cold, it's best to be preventative.

Address Negative Emotions at the Onset

As we read in the previous section, it's best to catch contagious emotions before they become a problem. This rings even more true when it pertains to uninspiring emotions; we have to nip them in the bud soon as possible. And what does nipping them in the bud entail? There will be moments when your team will be rife with anger or frustration, and managers will often ignore the negative emotion or simply pressure employees to keep their feelings at bay. The reason this is problematic is because it leads to employees feeling resentful toward management and can potentially cause job dissatisfaction.

Shitty feelings can be contagious. However, most managers have reported that they are not equipped to handle managing negative emotions because they haven't received proper training. According to a study, about 20% of managers reported that, in their entire careers, they never have had a single boss who effectively managed negative emotions. If this isn't scary to you, then you probably shouldn't be a manager. I was simply blown away by this statistic given how integral the role of the manager is. As a way to combat long-term spread of uninspiring sentiment, I recommend leaning into honesty by strategically confronting challenging conversations and situations head-on. The goal is to avoid escalation even in the face of discomfort.

"She probably thinks I'm a bitch," Jasmine recalled, regarding a direct report who was underperforming.

Honestly, she was not proactive. She had come from another team that was a lot more relaxed than ours and, generally, had a lot less work. She only did what she was told to do. I always had to make sure I was clear in what she needed to do. She was combative and perceived my feedback as being a micromanager.

At the time, we were working at an office in midtown. I had no idea when she started work—no idea if she started work early at a coffee shop. She would roll into the office around 10/10:30 a.m. when the rest of the team started at 9. She would randomly head for lunch for hours. I never knew where she was. It just made it challenging to assign stuff to her because I literally couldn't find her. Me trying to find her then became translated into being overbearing. I only found out she felt this way in her exit interview. She described me as an overbearing micromanager. Up until that point, I had no idea what she thought because she never brought it up in any of our one-on-ones. I tried so hard to engage with her—when I thought I was sharing encouraging feedback, it was ultimately perceived as being negative. I wish she would've just told me she felt differently. I just felt like I sucked at my job.

I've definitely been in Jasmine's position—we hope we're being helpful but it's received as being overbearing or, worse, as micromanaging. It's a tough act to balance but even harder when we're not fully aware of how the other person is feeling. Had Jasmine known of these negative feelings, she may have changed her approach to her report. It also makes me wonder: if the direct report harbored such strong feelings, why didn't she feel compelled to share them directly with Jasmine? Situations like this often leave so many questions on the table, with little to no signal on how they could have been addressed.

I worked at a design and tech studio and had a client who was so indecisive that it would take several rounds of review to make a decision. It didn't matter what type of work we showed him. I was convinced that we could've presented Picasso, and he would still find something wrong. One day, we had a design review, and one of our designers could not make the meeting. The client already seemed disgruntled, and that update sent him through the roof. He reprimanded my team and accused us of not prioritizing his work (mind you, we were several thousands of dollars over scope, but whatever). He kept repeating that he "didn't feel heard" despite us outlining our addressed feedback. We left that meeting feeling defeated and devalued.

It made me feel like my presence there wasn't as important as it should be, and yet, all I could do in the moment was try and reframe the conversation into a productive one. But inside, I was fuming. Unfortunately, this pattern of dissatisfaction and upset continued throughout the project. My majority of billed hours went to pacifying what essentially felt like a tantrum. Suffice it to say, I wanted to quit at every given moment. At a follow-up meeting, I gave the client feedback around giving feedback. More specifically, I told the client that being kind and clear in feedback would be more productive and helpful for the team. I said that I could address "fix x," but I couldn't necessarily address the emotional motivations and factors as to why the team wasn't feeling heard.

Suppose I was able to rewind that experience. The client could've kindly stated that he would rather reschedule to accommodate our designer. But if that even felt extreme for him, I would've gladly just taken a clear directive moving forward. Tonality is important during these moments. Err on the side of being clear and precise when trying to understand and resolve conflicting emotions. Don't add fuel to the fire by using a judgmental or assertive tone.

Nipping unproductive sentiment early on is important for employee retention. Studies have shown that employees prone to negative emotions tend to suffer poor physical and mental wellness, both on and off the clock. Employees feeling crappy about work will likely feel crappy about everything else. So how can we start getting ourselves out of the hole of uninspiring emotions?

Start asking questions. If you're unsure of how to deal with these icky situations, leaning into curiosity may help alleviate the problem. John Gottman's research at the University of Washington shows that blame and criticism reliably escalate a conflict, leading to defensiveness and disengagement. You can provide an open path for dialogue around a problem and solution by asking questions. Think about an individual's perspective and how they got there. Some questions and approaches include:

- Walk me through how we got here. Was there information I may have been missing?
- Ask a miracle question: If the problem was solved today, what would work look like right now?
- Do you need some time to reset away from the situation?

Asking a question will land better than asserting your opinion. Asking questions that require critical thinking on both sides may lead to a greater understanding of the nature of the issue in hopes of finding a resolution. By collecting this data, employees are better suited to handle challenging situations in the future, which ultimately maintains company growth.

Again, stopping uninspiring emotions can feel like fighting against a current, and it might be very tough to manage. But we can't let the current of uninspiring emotion drive where your team is. Be strategic in how you can diffuse the tension and work together in chipping away at any problems.

Be Accountable, Not Performative

When we think about the elements of trust, accountability ranks pretty high. For nondominant communities (POC, Black, LGBTQ, etc.), accountability rides a fine line between being performative and being sincere.

We've seen an uptick in being "performative" in the context of social justice. All around the country, employers have joined in the national conversation of allyship by putting out statements filled with platitudes around vague support. When employers engage like this, it becomes a question of whether they can walk the walk now that they're talking the talk.

When this act of using company statements to show support for anti-racism or any type of social justice movement without an action plan in place is supported by company leadership, it signals to a company that you can show an affinity for these things but not necessarily have anything to back it up. Performative allyship can have serious implications for building trust and advocacy for employees at both an organizational and managerial level.

"I just didn't think the company was targeting customers who look like me or even trying to attract talent that did," shares Sean. He was surprised to see his company repeatedly tout diversity and inclusion knowing how white their hiring pipeline has been. We've seen how this plays out: companies will roll out a performative statement around inclusion and support, yet there are no plans to shift the existing norms. This inherently creates distrust of the employer and its leadership at a macro level.

This idea of performative allyship and accountability doesn't just apply to social justice. It can happen in other facets of the workplace. An extreme example of this is when layoffs happen. I've been laid off twice, and it sucks. I've also been on the other side and had to let someone go. It's emotionally and mentally draining, and many feelings get hurt. Aside from Elizabeth's story, I've yet to hear about a layoff going well. A layoff may even be impending despite employees being told that "everything is fine" or "layoffs are not going to happen." I also know there are legal and financial implications around why the layoffs seem to roll out this way. However, the lingering mistrust in those moments tends to have a residual impact on employees. Cassandra recalls:

> Decision-making around COVID-19 was met with distrust of upper management. Our organization previously tended not to communicate things until they were all ironed out and finalized. Most notably, when it came to the fear of impending layoffs, very little was communicated to staff other than the fact that they may be a possibility. This fostered a lot of distrust with my manager, as I had no idea my staff was being laid off until the morning it happened.
>
> Additionally, surrounding the decision-making process of programming amidst COVID-19, there was a lot of confusion and mistrust of management as no information was communicated to us until they were finalized. This meant that we would often hear rumors of what would be happening with a program (i.e., that a program might be canceled) before hearing otherwise, or always remaining in a state of flux with decisions surrounding what was possible with COVID-19.

Employees desire sincere and genuine action from their employers. Following up and being accountable is part of that overarching need to develop an inspired work culture. Another way to look at it is that by being accountable, you're also exhibiting feelings of transparency and authenticity. Author of the critically acclaimed book *Start with Why*, Simon Sinek, shares this gem: "Transparency doesn't mean sharing every detail. Transparency means always providing the context for our decisions." Accountability and transparency work hand in hand to enable employees with a sense of trust and integrity.

While this level of accountability may feel unrealistic in bigger companies, Jasmine shares how her manager does a good job of affirming her concerns whenever their company is associated with less than favorable headlines in the news.

> *So, I work for a big company. When there's a misalignment in internal communication and what's happening in the news, I have always felt comfortable asking my manager to dig into what that situation is. Like, please help me feel better to understand where we stand as a company and what our values are. She'll respond with, "Let me bring this up to my manager." She'll follow up and send me clarification as to what happened and the situation. It's great that she does that and it helps me to not jump to conclusions.*

Regarding the topic of layoffs, I asked Jasmine how her company handled these tricky situations. Like many companies, she shared that they often framed layoffs as reorganization of the company. For context, when a company does a "reorganization," it's really just corporate talk for we're reshuffling folks because we're trying to save money. She mentioned that the company generally knows about layoffs about 90 days ahead of their termination date. Those who are directly impacted know about 60 days ahead of their termination date. This is done in part so that it allows employees to look internally for other roles but also gives them time to transition their roles as adequately as they can. I thought that was fascinating given that most of the layoffs I've been a part of have ultimately resulted in same-day notice of termination. Excluding any legal ramifications, I wonder if employees appreciate that type of heads-up. Or is it more emotionally manipulating? What do you think?

Accountability may not solve all of the trust issues a company has, but it does help a tiny bit to see companies stand by their own values. Context is key. No company is perfect, and I don't believe that we all think that our companies are going to be outstanding, but I do think there's a tiny part of us that hopes our companies are doing some good, and being accountable can be part of that tiny action of good.

Craft Psychological Safety

Psychological safety refers to the shared belief that employees can share or speak up without fear of rejection, embarrassment, or retaliation. Studies have shown that psychological safety allows for creativity by creating space for productive conflict and resolving the ability to voice suggestions, ideas, or concerns. With psychological safety, we become more open-minded, resilient, motivated, and persistent.

Managers are tasked with creating psychological safety for their direct reports, which means creating an environment that enables employees to share their thoughts and emotions freely.

For many employees, following through or being account-able can make a difference. Simply saying, "trust me" is not enough. Mars reflects,

> It shouldn't be about clearing your conscience. I wish people would just follow through. Like if you're saying, you are here to make me feel safe, follow through. You know I'm going through all these traumatic things. I'm processing this global trauma that I'm seeing being replayed on TV. Meanwhile, you're still giving me work and worrying about a deadline. As a manager, protect your employees.

Psychological safety takes time to build, but it can be easily destroyed. Unsurprisingly, not a lot of us are willing to engage in behavior that might have others negatively perceive our competence and awareness.

To craft psychological safety on your team, consider the following:

- Remember that feedback of any type should be about the situation and not the character of the person.
- Instead of being on the defense when friction arises, I recommend interrogating your feelings. Why are these feelings of defensiveness arising? Where did they stem from? Was this stuff that you've experienced before in a previous conflict?
- Even in the most heated arguments, generally, most parties want to walk away feeling happy. Keep in mind that you're still talking to another human with the same needs.
- Avoid blaming and shaming others. Shaming someone doesn't get them to stop
- Validate comments verbally and give credit.
- Be inclusive in interpersonal settings by letting your teammates know your working style or providing coaching to direct reports.
- Illustrate confidence and conviction without being rigid in your beliefs and work.

Ezra, who uses they/them pronouns, worked as an in-house creative at a company within the manufacturing sector. What started as a beneficial and even promising working relationship with their managers quickly turned into a hostile environment that prompted them to resign with no backup job or plan. In the beginning of their working relationship, Ezra's manager seemed receptive to their work process, which meant flexible hours. At one point, a personal issue required them to be out of the office for a few days. Like most managers, Ezra's began to increase their workload, but the amount of work started to concern Ezra, given their capabilities.

> My manager entered the meeting without reviewing the materials that I sent to discuss during this time. He took one look at the work that I'd been doing the previous day. He started outlining immediately all the changes that needed to be made. These suggested changes would increase the scope by adding a whole other day of work to do. I started pushing back on timing based on the requested changes, and he simply responded with, "Surely, it's not that much work. There's not that much going on here." [Since he was a micromanager,] he insisted on meeting later that day. I flagged to him that it'd be more efficient for me to go through all the changes and use the day to address them. He was insistent on the meeting, so I told him that if I were to keep the meeting, I would only be able to tackle four items on this list. He said, "Those are only four items." Nodding, I said, "Well, that's what I'm capable of doing right now in the next three hours, while the other requests will take more time and focus." I could see him getting worked up.
>
> My manager was emotionally chaotic. I felt that I had to have a steady emotional ground to field whatever emotions he was having in any particular meeting. He was very hot or cold. He was supportive and kind when things were going well. If things weren't going well, he would be passive-aggressive and usher in a sense of urgency without context. We had one-on-one meetings every day, twice a day. It just became stressful. I started having panic attacks [due to] the chaotic nature of my job.

Actions like the one above started to occur more frequently. It seemed that Ezra's manager refused to acknowledge Ezra's concerns and workload. They attempted to raise the issues with other people at work, but felt like they were being gaslit about their manager's behavior. Ezra continued to internalize the mixed messages they were receiving and, at points, started blaming themselves. Over time, Ezra's manager's polarizing behavior increased Ezra's annoyance to the point that they had to decide if they were going to stay. Every pushback was perceived by their manager as an attack, which resulted in Ezra feeling less motivated to do the work.

> *It finally clicked for me. I had an overly demanding manager [who was] a very intense person. I was just very naive and didn't have context. So I told myself if I have another shitty meeting where I'm left feeling disparaged or awful, I will give myself permission to leave. After making that promise to myself, I had another incredibly stressful meeting, and I said, "Okay, I made that promise to myself." The annoyance and difficulty just continued to make me feel uncomfortable.*

When we think about crafting psychological safety, it goes beyond being able to share personal life details; it includes sharing fear or hesitation around work. Most work environments ebb and flow with psychological safety. Sean explains how his new work environment has a sense of safety, but often, he still feels like a buffer is needed.

> *We were on a call with an internal recruiter [who was] completely off-mark in her recruiting approach. The point was slightly offensive, considering our backgrounds differ [in everything] from race to previous work experience. While she was talking, I was sending notes to my other colleague. I sometimes need someone else to be the buffer or the messenger because sometimes I think management will not like what I say when it comes from me even if I think they'll be receptive [overall].*

One way to assess and gather data on how employees approach emotions in the workplace is to develop a survey that asks them how they deal with tough emotional situations. The idea of an emotional survey was shared with me by the team at Coa, a venture-backed company that focuses on building emotional fitness for the workplace.

Specifically, the survey can ask questions, such as your preferred method of receiving tough feedback. Having a public source that gives managers and employees additional context about their teammates helps facilitate a more open and encouraging work culture. We did this exercise at a previous company I worked at and it did a few things for us: (a) highlighted where we were all similar, (b) became a point of conversation for teammates, and (c) helped us understand how certain teammates process emotions and feedback. The survey responses helped provide objectivity to something that felt very abstract.

Crafting psychological safety is an ongoing process that requires patience and folks who are committed to creating and maintaining the environment. Like all things, it's not one and done. You'll know when something doesn't feel right or doesn't resonate with your team. The world and the work that we do can be both stressful and chaotic, and providing a space to voice concerns, emotions, and anything in between gives us an opportunity to just breathe a little easier.

Develop Policy to Anticipate Emotional Needs

If you happen to be white, I'm sure as you're reading this you're like, "Oh wow, this is great information, but how do I actionize some of these things as a white manager?"

On a global scale, there are just "things" that happen, whether they be tragedies or events that we have to attend to and acknowledge. These things are often unexpected and there is no real way to know how to deal with tough feelings or situations. In the past two years, we've seen a lot—wars, Black Lives Matter protests, murders, a global pandemic—it's the unfortunate reality that we live in. One of the recurring points of feedback from managers and leaders alike is, "How do we address this?" It's a tough predicament for any company, regardless of race, gender, or religion.

I asked Dr. Gideon Litherland some of the best ways companies can try to provide some kind of provision around these tough situations as, unfortunately, tragedies can and will continue:

> I think because managers are not therapists, what they can really do is identify what concrete policies can be shifted to be more responsive or what policies can be made in anticipation of the emotional needs of the employees. I think the manager [and company] are the company-culture messengers and in [that capacity] they can set the tone. For example, is there a "No Questions" request [that's] honored within twelve hours? Is there messaging around the pacing of the projects? It's naming these policies not just once but multiple times. For example, do you say, "Expectations have shifted for the next month. Take the time you need to process?" It becomes [about] adjusting written policy and [managers] being the company-culture messengers that set the tone and pace of how responsive people should be. Hone in on policy and cultural messaging as some people find refuge in the work. So, sometimes they don't want to talk about these things. They want to go to work and do the work. They may not want the whole day to sit and process. They find safety in the work because there is prediction and safety.

In reflecting on Dr. Litherland's response, I think there is something to be said about developing or shifting policy that creates a sense of protection for employees regardless of whether or not the manager is emotionally supportive. In a sense, that's why a lot of policies exist: to protect marginalized communities. It is a double-edged sword to some degree—the idealist in me appreciates policy but is disappointed that we have to create a policy to begin with—but, do I agree that policy can create incremental impact? Yes.

I do think crafting any policy in relation to these types of scenarios should also include the context as to why it is necessary; it's not to guilt anyone, but to create an opportunity to provide a lens for another perspective. We can't speak about emotions without understanding the "why" behind it all.

There's a bit of reconciling that needs to happen on a company level when it comes to dealing with the unexpected emotional needs of employees. There is no perfect answer or solution into how anyone should navigate these situations. However, there are pathways to create a thoughtful strategy that can help alleviate some of the stress that work can induce on top of trying to process tragic situations. It's important for managers and leaders to be mindful of the implicit cultural messages they send, whether that be through policy or messaging.

When I think about what's actually feasible on both sides, I come back to the ideas of acceptance and action. Understand what we need to accept, and adjust the action to match. Every situation is different, no matter the narrative attached, and companies should view them as such. Conversely, individuals should also accept that companies may not have the perfectly timed or worded response to a situation right away, but there should be an action that an employee can opt into to help manage whatever the crisis may be. I think what becomes key for me in this is creating a framework of how we should think about and approach tough situations. Flexibility is needed to accommodate both individuals and companies in developing their own boundaries and at the very least a policy. To be honest, I'm not sure if I'm completely right but I do think it's worth thinking about.

Lean into Ambiguity with Curiosity

Throughout my interviews for this book, I flipped the question back to the cast. How should managers approach emotionally charged employee situations?

I'm sure by now you're also wondering, what do I do if (insert tragic event) happens but I have to meet a deadline? How can policy save that? To that I say, yeah, not sure if policy can help all the time. Each time I think I have an answer, I'm still left uncertain if it's the "right" thing. Maybe this is where the care comes in. Before we act, can we ask ourselves these questions?

- Would this person be so inconsolable that the deliverable would turn out shitty or incomplete?
- Does this person need work to cope? Have they expressed how they deal with stressful situations?
- Flip it back on them and grant autonomy. Is it possible to work together to come up with a solution that feels good to both parties?

We have to remember that processing any type of grief isn't binary or linear, meaning we aren't going to have a binary or linear response to a situation. When we start to hit this level of ambiguity, we should lean into our curiosity to lead us to the best next steps. Can we reflect even deeper and ask even more questions? Is this date flexible? Is the deadline self-imposed? Am I able to take on the work or can someone reallocate their time to support? Sean recalled a time where one of his direct reports came to him exhausted and on the brink of tears because her workload was overwhelming.

[In terms of managing that moment], I will say that as manager, the thing that I think I do the best is removing blockers for my team in place of adding more things to their plate. It's like how do I address this current plate? Having that in mind, we started to break down what she needed. [In this case], she felt like she wasn't getting the answers she needed from other teams or things that needed to be escalated. The thing is—it wasn't a "don't worry about this" and, more of, "how can I help you reprioritize?" And prioritizing those projects through both of our perspectives. She leaned into getting more muscle, aka me,

to help her move things through. I also think for her, it was also just being able to hear her out.

I think that I'm the type of person that just leaves mental space for fire drills in general [because of the nature of my job as a CX manager]. So I address that moment as a work fire and so I used that same energy that I would with other work fires to that person. There was some spill into other folks' plates in terms of reallocating work. More specifically to me and the other team—which ranged from determining what to delegate to others or just taking on the work itself. This direct report also took on a very convoluted project and tickets and, for some folks, it was a stretch opportunity. So for those moments—yes, it gave potentially more work to someone else but it was also about using that leverage as a growth opportunity for them. Or you just take the L as their manager.

When prompted about taking the L, Sean explained,"I am accountable and responsible for my team's performance, so it's like when you're the head coach [and, sometimes, you take the L] for your team."

Managers have the challenging role of not only translating cultural experiences from the company to their team but also vice versa. They're responsible (or at least, feel responsible) for translating their direct reports' emotions into the workplace.

Psychologist Dr. Will Osei is a consultant for various companies and works closely with DEI groups to develop culturally relevant and specific workshops. He shares,

Emotions often go the other way when we don't understand the experience. Pretending you know what your teammate is talking about when they describe their mental illness but wanting to run out the door because it's getting awkward. What should you do? Take a deep breath and get curious. If you are too emotional, you can't be curious. Your first question should be: Can I ask you some questions? Then, how can I best support you? How have you been supported well by previous managers? Finally, continue the conversation. Can we check in next week at 3 p.m.?

If you followed the previous step and were curious, the answer should be simple. Hopefully, your team member should have told you how to support them, or they have left the choice to you, or you'll ask again during the follow-up. Often people provide help that is not helpful. It's like coming out of a desert and wanting a big glass of water, but everyone keeps bringing you hot beverages. If we listen carefully and create opportunities to build trust, people will tell us how to help them, and then we don't have to guess.

I'm currently in grad school to become a therapist (I know, fitting, right?). If I had to pinpoint a common response across all my professors about how to best support someone it would be: "it depends." As you can imagine, "it depends" can feel infuriating as a response, especially in regard to how we can help someone. But "it depends" fuels our ability to think through our next action and to anticipate various responses/reactions. How do we handle these thoughts or feelings with a team member? A manager's role isn't to give advice. Their role is to help guide folks into their own resolution.

Similarly, I think we can take that same approach to these tough situations by leaning into curiosity and asking any and all questions. Can we zoom out from this particular moment and acknowledge there might not be an immediate solution? What if we looked at these moments as incremental shifts to discovering what works for both the employee and the team? Are we able to approach this situation with a bit more intentionality and not immediately enter in our own version of fight-flight-freeze? Are we able to enter these moments with nuance and look to individuals to help us draft the decision? It depends.

TOO LONG; DIDN'T READ

We covered a ton in this section! To reiterate, an employee code of conduct is typically an overarching guide on how to act properly in the workplace. Our version looks at the different characteristics and strategies we can leverage to develop the foundation of inspired work culture.

To summarize, we can approach building out an inspired work culture by doing the following:

- Developing cultural humility
- Modeling inspiring behavior
- Emoting (or not emoting) contagious feelings
- Addressing negative emotions at the outset
- Being accountable, not performative
- Crafting psychological safety
- Developing policy to anticipate emotional needs
- Leaning into ambiguity with curiosity

Remember that we want employees to get past surface acting to deep acting. Not everyone will feel comfortable going beyond what has been conditioned as appropriate emotional behavior.

So how do we use these guiding principles that we've outlined? Work closely with your team and develop a framework around these seven principles. Think about them as growth areas, and consider together what they mean. Use them as discussion points to start crafting what a framework or policy may look like for your company. The point of these principles is for your employees to leave feeling a little better about their company. We can't win if we're not right within. Companies can't win if their employees don't buy into their values or what they represent.

When we start foregrounding awareness and get into stages of contemplation and action, we can start to see what an equitable, empathetic work environment that takes into consideration cultural context and nuance could look like. Again, this is a framework that requires patience and openness. It will look different to everyone and that's okay. In fact, it should; we all manage feelings and cope differently. While I believe there is a systematic way of building these principles, I do think fluidity

in how we process and maintain this framework will be central
to what makes the process human.

PAUSE AND PONDER

- What are some examples of micro-moments that you
  could institute in your work environment?
- Are you able to describe the various "feeling rules" that
  you are part of? At work? At home? Reflect on how you've
  contributed to or hindered psychological safety at your
  workplace. Are there current policies in place that address
  moments of tragedy (personal or public)?
- Can a framework built around the aforementioned principles actually work? Why or why not?

Chapter 3 | Benefits Policy

Benefits tend to be the stuff that pulls you in as a candidate. Medical? Check. 401k? Check. Wellness stipend? Check. Benefit packages generally give employees a sense of how much the company is willing to invest in their employees' well-being and serve as a strong strategy for retaining top talent. Work culture acts in a similar capacity.

"There are better ways to empower your employees to deal with their emotions humanly. To be a good worker, you do not need to cut off your connection to your humanity and become a robot. You can still be a person," says Mars about the possibility of building an emotional culture.

We'll look at three areas in which an inspired work culture can have a positive impact on a company's bottom line:

1. Economic advantage and employee retention
2. Creativity and innovation
3. Avoiding bad publicity

Economic Advantage and Employee Retention

According to a Gallup study, there are economic advantages to showing emotion in the workplace. Data suggest that when organizations engage their customers and employees, they see a 240% boost in performance-related business outcomes compared to those without either. Fully engaged customers and employees drive market potential.

There is a downside companies should consider if they've cultivated a work culture that doesn't inspire or motivate. Research has shown that discounting or pushing aside negative emotions can cost organizations millions of dollars in lost productivity, disengagement, and dissipated effectiveness. In studies conducted by the Queens School of Business and the Gallup Organization, disengaged workers had 37% higher absenteeism, 49% more accidents, and 60% more errors and defects. Organizations with low employee engagement scores experienced 18% lower productivity, 16% lower profitability, 37% lower job growth, and 65% lower share price over time.

"I just want to create a place where people just like to work, first and foremost. I also know that if they stay, I know I have an incredible team that can generate awesome work that will inevitably allow us to raise our rate, and thus scale the business," says Logan as he thinks about his agency expanding. If you want employees to stick around, crafting a culture that is rooted in empathy, equity, and emotional fluency can be a major factor. Bradley reflects that his current work environment enables some level of psychological safety, a feeling he hasn't necessarily had before. Because of this, he's willing to stay and work there for a bit longer despite some of his own reservations regarding business strategy. When work is created haphazardly with emotional blinders and suppression, it can lead to increased turnover and a less than excited workforce.

Employees stay for more than the money. Studies have shown that cultivating work friendships is a huge reason why people tend to stay at certain jobs. Individuals with six or more workplace friends report feeling deeply connected to their companies. In a survey of 716 full time workers in the United States who had 6 to 25 workplace friends, nearly two-thirds said they love their company. The same study found that people with work friendships are less likely to accept an offer for a new job outside of their company, and the likelihood of their staying increases with the number of workplace friends they have. Sixty-two percent of employees with 1 to 5 work friends said they would reject an external job offer, and this increases to 70% for those with 6 to 25 friends at work. Beyond friendships, when employees have low morale, it decreases their overall work satisfaction and drives employee turnover faster. Reflecting on a past office environment, Kwanza said,

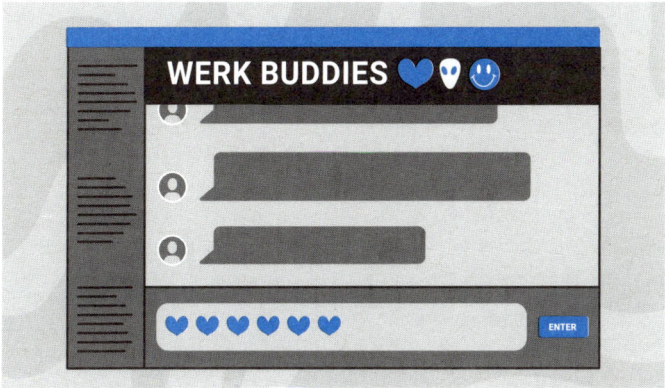

WERK BUDDIES 💙 👽 🙂

I was working in publishing and had transferred to a new department. It was similar work but with a different team and leadership. My last team thrived on camaraderie and collaboration with actual open-door policies and ownership of work. This new group operated in a trope of grinding away in silos to sustain the bottom line. It was a joyless division that mirrored the ladder-climbing yes-man who ran it, and no surprise, it never benefited the team.

Morale in my previous position came with the pleasure of doing my job, whereas now it was about keeping your job because it was the job to have and executives took advantage of that. This group put upon doing anything that made the head of the department supervisor look better. It wasn't like Wall Street, where you kill yourself for riches. These people busted their asses for the reward of having a place to work the next day. No one was happy there, but everyone was "happy to be there." I watched as a serial harasser was not fired but promoted and protected at the company. At the same time, leadership stifled other people's careers. It was so demoralizing to see what behavior was rewarded at the company [because] it wasn't hard work. My circumstances couldn't allow me to quit, so I gave up. I purposely let my performance slip so that I would get fired instead. It's pretty damn expensive to lose employees.

According to Gallup, the cost of replacing an individual employee can range from one-half to two times that employee's annual salary. The same report estimates that the United States loses a trillion dollars annually to employee turnover. The market continues to be competitive, offering employees more compensation and benefits.

As Gallup reports, "Fifty-two percent of voluntarily exiting employees say their manager or organization could have done something to prevent them from leaving their job." Businesses then have to account for direct costs including, but not limited to, higher competitive salaries, the cost of hiring recruiters, advertising, loss of hours interviewing, and the cost of training a replacement. Consider the hidden costs of employee turnover and onboarding: it'll still take weeks or even months before a new employee is in full productivity mode, meaning that your company is likely still losing money in the exchange. If you own a small business, the costs alone can significantly hurt your bottom line. So again, it is very expensive to lose employees and thus super important to think about an employee experience that results in retention.

Suppose a company prioritizes diversity and inclusion as a top business objective. It's not enough to diversify your pipeline. The work culture and environment must encompass psychological safety to support marginalized groups. Developing and retaining an inclusive environment is no longer just a checkbox in today's talent landscape but rather an opportunity to drive strong performance and business outcomes. According to a Deloitte study, millennials, who are rapidly becoming the majority of the workforce sector, are 83% more engaged when working in an inclusive culture.

The same study reports that "recruiting, retaining, and advancing diverse top talent is critical to remaining competitive. Companies with inclusive cultures have 22% lower turnover rates, 22% greater productivity, 27% higher profitability, and 39% higher customer satisfaction."

As Sean mentioned, "Why would I put in a referral for some-one who looks like me to an all-white working environment?" By investing in an inclusive work culture with psychological safety and caring embedded in its DNA, these types of work cultures are better primed to build a work culture worth staying in.

By developing an inspiring work culture, you're effectively creating an integral strategy for employee retention by nurturing and developing talent and leaning into intrinsic motivations to keep employees satisfied. Retention is no longer *just* about benefits; instead it's about crafting physical and mental safety for employees so that they can thrive. I work with early-stage founders, and when we talk about employee culture, I always ask: What do you want your employees to walk away with after their time here? Most say it's about the work they do and the people they work with. While monetary value is important, it's how we leave people feeling that stays with them.

Creativity and Innovation

Wharton management professor Michael Parke shares an excellent benefit of expressing emotions in the workplace: creativity. "We found that teams that have this environment where they feel comfortable sharing their genuine emotions with their team members, and they don't just ignore [emotions], but they work through them, not only do they come up with better ideas and insights; they get to the richer discussions as well," Parke said.

What we can gather from this is that the environment impacts the way we work. Environments that allow for authenticity to breathe generally create authentic work and work relationships. Further, Parke argues that often it's not even what is said to a teammate that lends itself to creativity, it's how the teammate expresses themselves and how the team receives it. This goes back to the idea of psychological safety, which allows for openness and for employees to be receptive to challenging ideas that may lead to new creative horizons or innovation.

I once worked at a design studio called the Lab and my team was in a challenging position that left us emotionally exhausted and prevented us from doing creative work. If there's one thing I know about this team, it's that they were a talented bunch of individuals. The Lab was upcoming and specialized in working with early-stage/pre-launch brands. However, we worked with a client who didn't feel confident in their own decisions despite any guidance from us. The client changed their mind frequently, gave conflicting feedback, and was emotionally draining. Our morale was low, and it was clear that we were disengaged with the work. To salvage the situation, Logan, the founder of the Lab, worked closely with the client to identify key friction points and areas of improvement. If you've ever been in therapy, that is exactly what the conversation felt like.

Unfortunately, I also had to be on this call. My role was simply to be a fly on the wall and to translate next steps to the team. After what felt like hours of back and forth on the root of the issues, the client, Logan, and I concluded that in order to save the project, we had to boost team morale. It was our reset conversation, but it was also a conversation we'd had many times before. This time around, we had to do things differently. At the start of our meeting, Logan addressed all the friction points and provided a new way to look at the work: Would we be proud? If the answer was no, was there anything we could do to improve it? Reframing this otherwise tough situation alleviated some of the uninspired feelings about the client and the work. What I realized later was that we lacked psychological safety in developing our ideas. We had to bring back that sense of safety to reinvigorate the team's creativity.

So I proposed: "How do we recover our psychological safety in order to create? What can I do to create boundaries between the client and us to protect that safety?" Hearing the questions made my team feel acknowledged and like there was action being done. Shortly after that, I felt the energetic, creative buzz from the team again. It was a slow buzz, but one that had been missing for quite some time.

With the support of an inspiring work culture, Elizabeth has evolved her role and built on her own skill set to support the company better.

> *[My leadership recognized that I was working well], so I became team lead because it was something I was already naturally doing. They let me be creative in what that meant past the initial requirements. I had the freedom to build processes that best help people, create programs, and work cross-functionally.*
>
> *Almost a year into the role, I know I have multiple opportunities. If I want to pursue management, I can. If I want to stay in the role, I can. If I want to go to another team to gain experience managing larger customers, I can. I'm slowly learning how to become a manager, connect with people, have tough conversations, and teach and coach. I'm constantly having conversations with managers and leaders about this. None of it is in the shadows. Also, last week I had terrible anxiety and called my boss sobbing, and he went, "Why are you trying to work? Sign off." And I did.*

By crafting an open and encouraging work environment, Elizabeth blended creativity and innovation into the current process, developing smarter ways to work and develop her talent. It's also important to note that her managers recognized her potential and developed her role in management. The consistency of open dialogue between her and management led to growth in her career trajectory and signaled to the company how to nurture and retain talent.

Emotional suppression, whether that comes as a result of a lack of psychological safety or poor team morale, leads to a decrease in creativity and innovation. Employees need to feel supported by their colleagues and management in order to evoke new ways of thinking that could lead to other positive results, such as career development or discovering efficient work streams. If a company strives to be at the forefront of the industry, employees are the real drivers of that mission. Simply put, if you want to transform your business from good to great, look at how your employees work with each other. Though it is complex, I believe that's a true signal of success.

Avoiding Bad Publicity

Every few months as I scroll on Twitter, I find myself reading a thread about the latest exposé of a toxic work company culture at an emerging, Instagram-famous brand. So-called pundits of the internet and startup world serve opinions on what it takes to be a CEO and how much suffering is acceptable as part of the startup grind. It's ridiculous and cringeworthy what people will say is justifiable for revenue gains. There are many companies with bad cultures, and an internet friendly brand with thousands of followers does not equate to a viable and sustainable work culture.

We've seen this play out in the media time and again with companies that have accepted bullying behavior to drive the business. We see leaders exposing themselves as incompetent or showing their lack of leadership qualities. Managers at these companies aren't positioned to galvanize and engage their teams but rather to focus solely on the executives under the helm of the founder.

We're seeing a pattern of breaking news stories covering poorly managed work environments that have left employees hurt, exhausted, or angry. A popular cookware brand found itself in the middle of a media frenzy when cofounder fallout led to the resignation of its six sole full-time employees. There were reports of bullying and unfair treatment. An employee in the creative department was quoted saying, "I would just walk out of meetings, sobbing, saying it's just not going to get better, she's not going to change."

As you can imagine, social media platforms fanned the flames. In a matter of days, the facade collapsed. The great brand became not-so-great. Reputations are fragile. A 2017 national survey conducted online by Harris Poll on behalf of CareerBuilder revealed that 71% of U.S. workers would not apply to a company experiencing negative press. The same survey shared that women were more likely not to apply to companies experiencing bad publicity than men. When a company receives bad publicity, its hiring pool and process often take a hit. Shame and embarrassment strike and impact employee morale, driving higher employee turnover and declining sales.

I spoke to a former employee of a very well-known bank that was catapulted into the spotlight due to significant trading losses. This individual was junior and was part of a cohort of other entry-level employees pulled into a room with a senior-level executive. One brave employee asked the top executive about the incident on the news. The executive quickly dismissed the question, uttering, "You don't even know what you're talking about." It was clear to this individual that this was not the place to slip up, considering the magnifying glass that was placed on the company during that time. Junior employees were expected to keep their mouths shut and hold their heads high despite the media storm.

"Looking back on the memory, this is a company of 100K+ employees, why on earth would I know anything about it? I held this company in such high regard only to realize how little they cared about us."

Poorly handled media crises shroud the company in further judgment and impact how employees start to view themselves. We noted previously that our work identity is an inherent part of presenting ourselves. When we are associated with something deemed in the public as harmful or negative, it can impact our output at work. The constant confrontation from both the media and inner circles can be difficult to manage since both require our attention.

After a while, employees may not have the emotional capacity or mental bandwidth to properly reengage with the work. While we know that publicity can be short-term, we know that the news cycle or Twitter feeds will continue to relentlessly discuss a company's downfall. It's what these platforms thrive on: hypercritical analyses of people, things, and places. Yet, we consume it all. More directly, past, present, and future employees can and will see it all as well. Companies are better served avoiding these types of confrontations and at the onset, determining what kind of companies they want to be. Employees are evangelists; they have the potential to be the best broadcasters of how a company truly functions and behaves.

TOO LONG; DIDN'T READ

At the core of this benefits policy, we recognize a pattern on the impact of employee retention. Take note of how many strategies are cultivated to make people feel emotionally and physically safe. It's not enough to create platitudes, hoping that cultural shifts occur within office walls. It's about committing and developing policies and behaviors that enable inspiring action while also allowing flexibility. We live in a highly complex world—there could be a million ways to develop a path of action, but companies must be open and receptive. It's a full circle—how we treat employees is how they treat each other and how others perceive the company.

PAUSE AND PONDER

- Reflect on your previous work experiences. What were some of the reasons that you wanted to stay? What made you want to leave? Let's say you're in the interview process for a new company. During the process, you receive a text from your close friend with an article about the company's CEO. The article mentions how the CEO tends to be

rather aggressive to employees and reportedly treats the company's customer experience team poorly. Does this new information impact your decision to move forward in the interview process? If so, why? If not, why not?
- Were you surprised to learn about the hidden costs of hiring new employees? If so, what was surprising about the costs? If not, does it serve as motivation to develop stronger employee retention strategies?

Chapter 4 | The Catalyst for Change

We naturally jump to examining executive leadership when talking about influencing work culture. It makes sense, the top-down trickle of change is common among all organizations and when we see executive leadership, we see the embodiment of the company. These are the people we see in the public eye, the ones who share insight and wisdom on stage and on screens. We see them on panels and giving keynotes. They're also probably the ones writing a book about emotions. However, the biggest catalyst in shifting emotional work culture isn't executive leadership, it's middle management. Yes, I mean people like me and you.

Reflect on your career as a manager. Do you remember how you made people feel at work? Would you consider yourself an integral part of someone's employee experience? If the answer is yes, then yes, you are a major catalyst for change. Managers are a central source of helping employees manage and regulate emotions at work. For all the times I've been frustrated or excited, I usually have my manager as a springboard for my feelings. Throughout my career, my managers have been central to my experience and influenced a lot of my perception of a company. They are, in essence, caretakers of teams. As a manager, I willfully accept that a lot of my role is dedicated to ensuring that my direct reports feel heard and seen. This is not explicitly asked of me so why do I do it? What provokes me to instill this sense of nurture? The next section focuses on the role of managers and why they can become change makers in a work environment.

A Manager Is the Quarterback of a Team

While I don't know much about football, I've been told several times in my career that my role was to "quarterback" a project.

For those unfamiliar with American football or the concept of a quarterback (aka me), a quarterback is considered the most important position in the game. They're the brain and heart of the team. The quarterback calls the plays, initiates action, and handles the ball. Like a quarterback, a manager is often the central source for the team. It is generally the person who oversees development and execution. A formal definition describes middle managers as the bridge between individual contributors and executive management. They manage their team's career progression, communicate decisions from executive management, and adjust workflows, processes, and priorities to align with overall business goals. So, yeah, a quarterback.

Research has shown that a manager's engagement with employees influences inspiring workplace behaviors such as mentoring and creating opportunities for empowerment. A good manager can also recognize talent, identify a person's uniqueness, and transform it into a results-oriented performance. For a manager to recognize and identify an individual's talent or uniqueness, they start with the simple interaction of getting to know the individual.

In Kim Scott's *Radical Candor*, she emphasizes the need for managers to care personally. She writes: "It's about giving a damn, sharing more than just your work self, and encouraging everyone who reports to you to do the same. It's not enough to care only about people's ability to perform a job. To have a good relationship, you have to care about each of the people who work for you as human beings."

By nurturing their direct reports, managers learn a person's strengths, learning style, and what the company does to support them. By understanding these levers, the manager can appreciate the individual and craft development plans that cater to that person's strengths. Managers are tied to employee growth as they tend to be in charge of employee feedback, so their advocacy affects an employee's general outcome and well-being. In essence, managers set the tone for the rest of the team because they are closely linked to their direct reports.

Within the manager–direct report relationship, there is a power dynamic that must be considered. Unlike a CEO–employee relationship, the manager–direct report relationship is a lot more precious. I spoke to a former marketing manager of a higher education platform who remembers the feeling of being welcomed and safe to present as herself at work. "I didn't know what emotional safety was until I met my manager and was welcomed into this environment. I felt I never *had* to share my identity but felt welcomed to do so. My teammates knew I was queer. I felt safe being able to share more of who I am."

All this to say, managers are important because they are the ones who have to build bonds and relationships with direct reports. Going back to the sports reference, they are the quarterback and the coach simultaneously.

Managers Are the Translators of Company Culture

Middle managers cultivate how teams see, hear, and feel company culture. Many managers are often the nucleus of a cross-functional work stream. Their jobs are often to interpret and translate the broader strategic plan to different departments and teams, speaking in different business languages to ensure everyone is on the same page. To be an effective manager, they have to act and speak differently to accommodate these various teams. Think about that a bit. A manager needs to have the ability to understand, interpret, and then relay information to different teams, meaning they have to

build an arsenal of different languages to ensure that the message is received. Wow. Isn't that amazing? It's no wonder that managers are so embedded in an employee's work experience.

Research has shown that managers have the most significant influence on the employee experience. In organizational psychology, R. M. Kanter's structural empowerment theory supports the impact of management. This theory highlights the importance of a leader's behavior as foundational to shaping and enhancing work experiences and employees' work life. Managers are the drivers of how teams adopt change and execute the company vision. On the *McKinsey Talks Talent* podcast, McKinsey leader and talent expert Bryan Hancock speaks about the vital role many middle managers play in their organizations:

> Take, say, a leader of a technical competency, whose role is to define what good looks like, shape learning journeys, shape career development, aggregate year-end feedback—not to be a bottleneck but to adopt the mindset, "What I'm here to do is to coach, support, lead." When managers spend the majority of their time coaching and leading, we see real returns.

Overall, 76% of employees agree that their managers set the workplace culture. Yet 40% of employees surveyed say their bosses frequently fail to engage them in honest work conversations. In comparison, 36% believe their supervisors don't know how to lead a team and 58% of those who left a job because of workplace culture cited their manager as the reason behind their decision.

This data tells us that middle management holds a lot of power. Their actions impact how teams act and feel and have a ripple effect within a company. So if your manager doesn't create the space for you to be open, chances are, you will not be open in the work environment. With the same lens we view emotions through, inspiring and uninspiring, let's also view managers.

An inspiring manager has the ability to manage their emotions consistently. It's not that they are withholding or suppressing, it's a matter of developing self-awareness that can effectively help them process. What does it say to have a manager who can discuss stressful situations? Or a manager who can identify emotions during social interactions and could respond in an empathetic way? What does it say to have an empathetic manager? Logan recalls one of his managers:

He was an amazing manager for engineering. He was great at explaining topics and leveling up the staff. He offered a lot of support when it came to venturing into new spaces. Made learning new concepts fun and interesting. He was often thinking about how to push the bounds of what we were doing even if it was just a new way to write code. He wasn't great with resourcing, but I learned a lot.

What I heard from Logan was the value of patience, exploration, and support. Not to be cliché, but people remember you by how you make them feel. In Logan's case, he felt supported and encouraged. Not everyone is meant to be a manager. It's a hard and complex role in an organization. It's not enough to be a great contributor and be good at your previous role. Being a manager takes resilience and a ton of emotional awareness and fluency because this role requires interfacing with other employees daily. What we know is that being a manager is part doing the job and the other part figuring out how to do it.

What are the qualities that make for an uninspiring manager?

"I watched coworkers taking on extra work diligently over delivering quality, only to be passed over for promotion by some new kiss-ass with no experience. This unit's managers couldn't bother to know a third of the department was vegan and vegetarian when ordering catering for a very awkward obligatory holiday party," reflected Kwanza.

I once had a manager who told me they were a bad manager. I laughed it off, but I felt what it meant to have an absent manager over time. There was no one to share ideas, explore work, and make decisions with. It felt like roaming aimlessly in an open field, hoping for a sign to guide me. Often, uninspiring managers are not equipped with the proper resources to fundamentally do their job. Or sometimes, some people are just not meant to manage teams. I think we have to be okay with that and understand that career growth does not necessarily mean a path to management. What we want to avoid is having uninspired managers inaccurately portray that the workplace culture is uninspiring. We'll talk more about the limitations and challenges that managers face a bit later.

Managers Catalyze Change

Studies have found that middle managers tend to think beyond traditional notions of self-interest (individual power, economic value, and social status) and about organization-related identities, meaning middle managers think about the organization as a whole. Another way to frame the concept of an organizational identity is the idea that "the company's success is also my success."

At their core, managers are people managers. Keeping in mind the group mentality, managers hold the special ability to move and motivate people. When we define the ability to "move someone," we identify that this individual can drive strong emotions in another individual or a group. Therefore, an employee's motivation (or demotivation) is intrinsically tied to their manager.

The manager's role requires caring deeply about their direct reports: understanding strengths, weaknesses, and anything in between. A manager should leverage their findings about their own direct reports to build a team culture and expand. As senior executives set the tone for a company, managers set the tone for the team and how everyone treats each other. Developing and maintaining standards of how we treat each other can influence an employee's journey at a company for many years to come. I had a manager who once said, "What we do with the first ten employees is what the next 100 employees will see."

Current Limitations

In understanding the complex and significant role of the manager, I think we also have to be aware of the limitations managers face from both an inter- and intrapersonal perspective. We need to have high expectations of managers; however, we also need to understand the clear limitations to an individual manager's growth. To effect change, companies also have to improve the path to becoming a manager—think developing cultural humility, proper training, and identifying if an employee is meant to be a people manager.

Balancing the role as a manager and a direct report.

Managers are in a tough position, both emotionally and within the organization. They're quite literally in the middle, toggling between being a report for senior executives and being a manager to others. As you can imagine, the constant context switching from direct report to manager leaves many employees emotionally, mentally, and physically exhausted. On top of the context switching, managers are also responsible for their team's emotional well-being. Quite simply, it's a lot. I often found myself perplexed during my one-on-one with my direct report because I felt like I was constantly context switching at the last minute. Meaning I would go from one meeting focused on one topic and then having to switch my attention to my direct report, often with little to no time to decompress or set myself up properly with my report. Sean reflects on a period where he was stuck between having a difficult direct report and being potentially viewed as a bad manager with the guidance of a not-so-great manager.

> I was just fresh off becoming a new manager and I had one direct report who was extremely needy in the day to day. By that I mean she would ask a ton of questions but wouldn't take initiative. She was a bad listener even when I did give feedback or tried to help. It just required a lot of attention.
>
> On top of this tension, she also had undisclosed health conditions that would require her to be out of office frequently and often. Because of that, it felt like I couldn't really ask her for anything and it became more of an issue with my direct manager at the time because it was impacting overall productivity. I think in the midst of it, I had to play peacemaker between my direct manager and my direct report because it started to get into HR and legal territory [because of the Family Medical Leave Act], which my direct manager had to handle [since we were a younger company at the time and so HR was literally one person]. What made this more difficult was that my direct report felt like my manager did not take her concerns seriously. So as a peacemaker, I felt like I had to make sure that my direct manager understood where my direct report was coming from.

During the whole process, there was a lot of internal conflict. It's like—I want to take care of this person who is on my team but also this person and I don't get along and we don't see eye-to-eye on the work itself either. But her well-being is the most important. So it's questioning how do I take care of her, but also how do you play emotional defense when things start to fall out of scope, which felt like that was the case regarding her condition. For me, as a new manager at the time, I was pretty stressed. I still had goals to meet with the team but then I have this person who is not only unavailable but is also inconsistent for reasons you can't legally touch.

It was a drawn-out process. I had a decent relationship with my direct manager at the time but I did not like her. She had a history of mishandling employee situations and was overall absent as a manager. But I knew I had to approach her out of necessity and because I didn't know how to handle the situation. At a certain point, because the process was so drawn out, I was phoning it in and performing empathy. I wasn't as empathetic because I was burnt out by the situation, which just made dealing with both my direct report and my manager more draining.

Sean's story illustrates how sticky being a middle manager can be. This doesn't even touch on the fact that Sean probably also had individual contributor (IC) work to manage on top of managing situations like the one outlined above.

Taking a step back, if we were Sean—what options could we have leaned into? Why or why not would they work/not work?

Option 1   Instead of managing up, what if Sean had strongly "sided" with his direct report?

Option 2   Despite his manager's inconsistent history of support, what if Sean "sided" with his manager and their approach to managing his direct report?

Option 3   What if Sean escalated the situation to another manager instead of his own manager?

If we went down the path of option 1, my first gut reaction would be to consider optics for the rest of his team. How does this look to others? What does this evoke for his team when they know that his report is not contributing to the broader team goals? As a follow up to this thought, does he address this imbalance to the team? While we want to advocate for our employees, we do need to consider the ramifications of doing so. This starts to get into sticky territory in terms of what is then recognized as "fair" or "balanced" across teams.

If we decided on option 2, similar to option 1, it's also a game of optics. What are we implying when we take this action in support of our managers? Does this imply that we're not strong employee advocates? What are we hoping to evoke from "siding" with our manager? The fact that Sean's manager has had an inconsistent history should also be a factor when we consider how we might want to present to our team. Are we implying that we may share the same values? Is that actually true of Sean?

In the case of option 3, some managers are not huge fans of employees going to someone above them. Despite this, I think it's always important to get a third party opinion especially when it feels like you're stuck. Generally, this could come in the form of your People Ops team or a skip-manager that you trust. In other words, managing up. If you decide to manage up, take note of a few things—who is this person to my direct manager? What is my goal by escalating this to them? What could they escalate or accelerate for my direct report? At the heart of it, does this benefit my direct report in any capacity?

While these options may still lead you down the same road (in Sean's case, a drawn-out process), at least you were able to evaluate your options and hope to find a solution that at least slightly benefits your direct report. During this time period, I also hope you find your own support system—while you are in charge of your team, you shouldn't also lose your sanity. If your manager isn't the most reliable person (as in Sean's case), seek support through your own trusted circle of folks.

It is mission-critical to understand the fundamentals of a manager's role and how intricate and pivotal it is to the work environment. They hold so much power and influence in ways that executive leadership cannot tap into by proximity within the organization. Questions we should ask:

- Knowing the power of managers, how can we bolster them in our organization to give them more flexibility to be managers?
- Are we assessing and reassessing our training programs to give managers the best type of training?
- What do we want our managers to reflect and translate to others?
- Do we need to bring in a third party e.g., skip-level manager) for support?

Ultimately, managers are put in the crossfire of trying to satisfy two major key stakeholders: their manager and their direct report. How can they manage to satisfy both? Is it worth bringing in another third party that can help diffuse tension and provide some relief? There are no clear answers here, but I think we can go back to leaning into curiosity to at least create some breathing room and maybe some brain power to develop an interim working solution.

Lack of management training.

Not many managers are properly trained to manage and understand the implications of their role. "There is a pervasive lack of leadership management training happening when people are moving into management," says Scott Miller, executive vice president of thought leadership at FranklinCovey and author of *Everyone Deserves a Great Manager: The 6 Critical Practices for Leading a Team*. Jasmine recalls her first experience as a manager:

When you get promoted, you start to manage people. You take your personal experience and what you like and what you don't like about your previous managers. I've learned that it can be biased—the way you like to be managed may not be how someone else likes to be managed. There was no formal training when I was promoted [to my first managerial role]. I had to think about what I did as an assistant and use that to train [my team]. People don't realize how difficult it is to manage. It's not even the technical aspects, it's all the interpersonal stuff you have to worry about. The communication piece. Four promotions later and at a different company, I finally got formal leadership training. I found it well done [with] lots of focus on personalities and communication.

I've been in plenty of leadership seminars catered to building up managers, but rarely do I see ones on the implications of how managers can influence a company's emotional culture. We're not trained in "soft skills," such as the ability to navigate emotional intelligence in interpersonal work relationships. Managers hold the key to unlocking the potential of culture.

"That's the thing—they don't tell you that when you become a manager. As a manager, you're invested and committed to someone else's growth. It's my job to ensure that I stay invested in this person's growth. That means that the feedback I'm giving you is meant to be helpful and insightful. If I can't deliver, then it's my job to tell you why not. I feel really bad when I can't make a change for my team. It's stuff that is above my pay grade, but it doesn't make me feel better that I couldn't make it happen," shared Jasmine.

I think we also need to candidly call out that a middle manager's ability to impact real change (e.g., promotions) is always going to be somewhat limited; rather, let's focus on how managers should do the best that they can to ensure that their employees feel cared for. While we may want to help folks get to the proverbial next level, sometimes it's truly out of our own control, but what we can hope to do is establish and build trust with our employees because that in itself will deliver results.

A goal of companies should be to look at middle managers and see them as ambassadors of their emotional values. While this starts at the top, the focus is on how these messages get translated. How can we bolster our managers to receive emotional training?

Lack of diversity and the cycle of the "like us" mentality.

Another limitation that I haven't seen addressed in many studies is the lack of racial diversity in middle management. I often wonder what the current demographic makeup of managers looks like. Which population of folks are we basing a lot of our data around? According to the U.S. Bureau of Labor Statistics, in 2021, of the sixty-four thousand people who identified as a manager, 78% identified as white, with Hispanic/Latino as the second largest group at 10%. What does that tell us? It reinforces the idea of professionalism being dictated by white culture and that the "like us" mentality—the hard-wired desire to engage or hire people who look and act like you—prevails. We rarely see non-white executives.

Still, it illustrates even further that we're missing a huge cultural component in defining management and, essentially, leadership in the workforce. When we look through the lens of the majority, we lose cultural nuance and perspectives that enable change, growth, and, more importantly, impact on the bottom line.

Managers are not therapists.

Despite all the things that a manager does and the skills they need to have, managers are not therapists and lack the fundamental training and skills to help employees manage and deal with emotions as a therapist would. It's not realistic to expect a manager to have developed a high emotional IQ, which is the ability to assess and manage emotions. Having a high emotional IQ is certainly desired, but managers don't necessarily always have the proper training to help regulate and manage emotions.

Dr. Litherland shares that managers, in the context of their work, are similar to counseling supervisors. The role of a counseling supervisor is to help strategize with the therapist-in-training and to provide consultation as an expert. In the field, countertransference (when a therapist projects emotions or feelings toward the client) happens a lot. An example of countertransference is when you treat a client similarly to your sibling because they remind you of them. If a supervisor can sense that a therapist is beginning to intertwine their own "stuff" during their one-on-one, it is the responsibility of the supervisor to call out the need to work through the therapist's feelings separately with their own therapist. I asked Dr. Litherland how managers can leverage that mentality and articulate it to employees. He shared the following as an example of what a manager can say, "I really appreciate you sharing all of this with me. I think this is really important stuff to work through and I just don't have the professional skills to help guide you through this really tough scenario. I am more than happy to direct you to resources or to our people ops team to see how we can find a way to."

In digesting all that Dr. Litherland shared, I concluded that a lot of what I thought I knew about people management needed to be rewired. I couldn't help but think about what my friend, Jorge, said after I shared these findings: "How do we as up and coming business leaders make sure we don't repeat the sins of our past bosses in a society that makes you feel you have to be a dick to be effective?"

Here's to finding out how not to be a dick.

Recognizing empathy as a double-edged sword.

With all the talk of feelings, I have to mention how empathy plays a role within the manager and direct report dynamic. Cassandra reflects on how empathy may have clouded her judgment in addressing a direct report's performance.

> I'm currently in the midst of putting a direct report, let's call her Amber, on a performance improvement plan (PIP). For context, there was a point where Amber was my strongest report. At the start of last year, there were moments where her work deteriorated a bit but I didn't address it head on. Over time, she started to open up to me about her personal life, more specifically, how she was having to care for a family member due to a medical condition. It all started to connect—why her work was declining, why she wasn't consistent. It honestly felt like a breakthrough like, "Great, tell me what's going on so I can figure out how to help." It's been almost a year now, and not much has changed, hence why she's on a PIP.
>
> When I look back at what I could do differently—sometimes, I think my empathy and compassion got in the way of communicating clearly, especially when I had to give her constructive feedback. By that I mean, I would give feedback but layer on my projected sense of empathy by sandwiching something like "I know you have a lot going on, and want to be mindful of that!"
>
> In some ways, I felt like I was therapizing her. When I delivered the news that she was on a PIP, she responded with, "Yep, totally makes sense. I saw this coming." But she soon followed up with, "respond best with direct feedback, don't beat around the bush." Which made me realize I beat around the bush. [When I say] I beat around the bush, I mean as a result of me trying to empathize, I didn't actually give her what she needed from me. In the past, I've received and been given feedback through the feedback sandwich, which is affirm, feedback, and affirm. Only later did I realize she didn't need the affirmation or my empathy, but she needed my direct feedback. So I've been employing more of that in our daily check-ins. But it does make

me uncomfortable—I'm going from cushioning feedback to just being up front about it.

Cassandra's story made me wonder where the lines of empathy begin and end for managers. Empathy can be a double-edged sword—when you employ it, generally, it's received with effective impact. It's a feeling we often desire from our own managers. However, can there be too much empathy that it renders itself unproductive? Again, I think we have to reconcile what ideals we hold around empathy and the actual reality we live in. I also think it's important to call out that having empathy is different than avoiding having difficult conversations. In the case of Cassandra, we see how she may have confused empathy with avoiding conflict or not wanting to hurt someone. You can be very empathetic and still end up hurting someone else.

Get clear on empathy and what it means for you. When you say empathize, does that mean you are taking on the other person's perspective? Are you experiencing a similar intensity of emotion to the other person? Or are you compelled to take action? Often, when we say we empathize, it usually is indicative of the first definition—you can put yourself in someone else's shoes. However, just because you can does not mean it precludes you from feeling pain, disappointment, or even anger.

Empathy shouldn't mean you're detached from your current circumstances. Deadlines will happen. Life will happen. But can we be flexible to a reasonable extent? Can we expend a decent amount of energy and empathy to a reasonable extent?

Sean realized he needed to draw a line in his own empathy when he felt like he was being performative. In reference to managing the situation with his former direct report that had poor performance and required to be out of office frequently, Sean reflects:

I would say in the context of that moment, I did truly feel like I was performing empathy as in conveying a literal performance. I felt like I was putting on the mask of empathy rather than actually

Chapter 4

empathizing. I think there comes a point because the situation dragged on for so long [in dealing with HR and my direct manager] that I just had to perform for optics' sake during our one-on-one. I wasn't as really empathetic as I was initially and was burned out by the situation. Otherwise, I would say that I'm pretty genuine about my empathy when it comes to my reports. But yes, that time did test my ability on how much I could empathize.

There's a delicate balance in determining how much compassion and empathy one can give to another person in the context of work. We don't want to hit compassion fatigue to the point that it feels inauthentic to us, but we still have to remain at least understanding. To Cassandra's point, we also don't want our own empathy to cloud our judgment and decision-making. So what do we do?

Working with empathy is going to require trial and error and trusting our instincts. As Dr. Will Osei notes,

Boundaries should be set from the outset of a crisis, and as a manager, you should take the lead in setting them. The initial conversation should be ended by selecting a date and time for a check-in. The only exception should be during an active crisis (e.g., on the way to the ER). I recommend at least doubling the number of 1:1 contacts. If you typically meet once a week for a 1:1, add a second more minor check-in during the week. You'll then be ready for unexpected events like a dip in performance.

When performance starts to dip, you need to *call out the elephants in the room* and be curious. You can frame it as, "Hey you've been missing a lot of deadlines and I want to know if there's a way I can better support you."

Watch out for certain signals in their response that may indicate where they are emotionally:

Prove-It Mode   "I'm sorry, I will catch up this weekend. Just give me a few more days!"

Feeling Equals Facts   "I can't do anything right. I've been trying so hard to keep it all together, and now you're upset at me too!"

Pretend Mode   "Yeah, I'm a little behind. It's no big deal the client isn't even checking the files anymore."

Here are some responses to tackle the above:

Prove-It Mode   "Okay let's take a deep breath before we start throwing out solutions. Can I understand what caused you to miss the deadlines? Are you still managing things for your family? Have you talked to HR about taking some time off?"

Feeling Equals Facts   "It's okay. I'm not mad, I'm worried about you. You said you have to keep it all together but maybe you don't. It might be time to put your family first. Can we talk about the options?"

Pretend Mode   "I know you're going through a lot, but do you understand what exactly I'm upset at? I know it seems like the client is not checking, but when they do, how do you think they'll feel after paying for us to complete it? How might you feel? If you're approaching burnout, let's dissect that together and see where we can alleviate some of that tension."

The key is not to fear misunderstandings. This wonderful thing happens when we guess wrong about people's thought processes. They correct us, and they don't even notice most of the time. We all have a deep need to be understood, and if we can manage our emotions and stay curious, we can find the correct answer to most situations.

Similar to when we deal with ambiguity, I think we have to offer ourselves first a little grace (because this shit is hard), and, second, some type of internal checks and balances. Can we ask ourselves questions like:

– Have I given and exhausted any and all resources to this person?

- Have we established any type of timeline to potentially reconnect or re-examine outstanding work?
- Which levers can I control? Have I leveraged them adequately enough to ensure work is complete?
- Is this person experiencing challenges beyond my control?

If I had to take a guess, so much of this is also built into our own personal anxiety and desire for control because there are many factors on the line. But, if you can take a step back, and start to provide yourself clarity on what you can and cannot control, that might give you some guidance on how much you can extend your empathy to your team. Unfortunately, we can't lose sight of the fact that it is still work, so outlining your internal boundaries and limitations is going to be key to developing your own internal checks and balances.

TOO LONG; DIDN'T READ

Managers are crucial and integral to a company's success and culture. For an effective and deliberate cultural change, we have to empower managers to foster relationships built on emotional fluency and competency in order to see change within the organization. They are the keys that unlock the very act of being able to emote in the workplace. When we think about the feeling rules, we should see how these rules are enforced or challenged. Who are the ones enforcing it? Who are the ones challenging? Implementing change is hard and it is rooted in a fundamental shift in how people will be received.

Far too often, managers go into these complex roles with little to no experience in developing and managing the feelings of others. Without proper education and skill sets, managers are often left on the shit end of the stick juggling multiple responsibilities. It's easy to see how the top can influence the company, but rarely is it seen how the middle creates impact.

- How would you describe your manager's job description? Does that description include managing emotions? If so, is it clear? Is it implied?
- Are there any roles or positions in a company that take on similar responsibilities as a cultural translator?
- Reflect: Are you currently a manager? What are you doing or not doing to develop bonds and relationships with your direct report(s)?

Chapter 5 | Career Development
"Choose Your Own Adventure" Scenario

Navigating these scenarios can be daunting, but I'm here to help. We've developed a "choose your own adventure" format with a few familiar employee vignettes. As in life, the emotional moments that are drummed up at work are often unexpected. We can only think about how we might respond to a situation, but we have very little control over how things actually go. These scenarios are inspired by real stories and illustrate different vantage points in approaching situations. Take note of your initial responses as well as how your responses may change over time. There are no wrong answers here. View these exercises as an opportunity to reflect and take account of your biases and thoughts when approaching feelings at work. Keep in mind these considerations when evaluating these scenarios:

- Is this reflective of what I believe an inspiring culture supports?
- If it's not reflective of what I believe an inspiring culture supports, where do these ideas/biases stem from? Do I want to challenge them?
- Am I taking into account my own previous experiences? If so, what am I feeling in recognizing the familiarity?
- On a scale of one to five, one being "not comfortable at all" and five being "very comfortable," how would you rate your comfort level in managing the suggested situation?
- What kind of feeling rules am I enforcing? Are they influenced by my own beliefs? Or the company's?

Again, there is no right answer. In real life, a lot of these moments happen on a continuum, and you can change your mind at any time. The goal here is to help you prepare and develop a mindset of openness and receptiveness crafted by inspiring feelings and an emotional work culture.

Finally, I would love to leave you with the guiding principle of treating others how they would like to be treated. Ultimately, cultural humility works when we are open to understanding and gaining perspective as to how people would like to be treated (and seen and heard).

Situation 1

You notice that one of your direct reports, Ramon, looks disgruntled during a meeting. Shortly afterward, he asks if he can chat with you for a few minutes. You agree and schedule a quick check-in. During your check-in, he starts to explain what occurred with another coworker. You gather that he had supported the team lead during this project and, in that meeting, realized that the project lead used all of his research without notifying or crediting him. His frustration slowly becomes anger as he speaks. He begins to spiral from venting to talking negatively about the project lead. What do you do?

Choice A   Ask Ramon for a pause and kindly ask him to refrain from speaking negatively about the other coworker. Given how riled up he is, you suggest that Ramon take a walk, and you will plan to regroup shortly. You tell him that you understand his frustration, but it might be best for him to brainstorm with a clear mind to find a solution. You suggest he take up his frustration directly with the project lead.

Choice B   You let Ramon vent. After all, we've all been frustrated by a coworker and wished our manager would just let us process and vent. You know he worked hard on the project, so you understand his anger. While you're actively listening to Ramon, you begin to think about how you can help course correct. As he gets angrier, you remind him that he needs to take action. So, you call in the project lead to help mediate and try to put out this fire fast.

If You Chose A   You want Ramon to feel his feelings. Still, you don't want to reinforce the behavior of talking negatively about another coworker. You know Ramon does not mean any harm, but you don't want this to become a repeating behavior with any of your reports (and they are both your reports). After assessing Ramon's issue, you find it best to let Ramon process and develop on his own how he should bring his concerns up to his team lead.

If You Chose B   You're mindful of what it means to process and emote anger, especially for someone who is a person of color, but you don't want the anger to linger. You believe in radical candor and find it best to have Ramon and the lead figure out their feelings openly. You can act as a mediator if necessary. Sometimes, things can get hard but you want to explore what it means to figure things out openly and normalize tough conversations with each other. Again, your role is to help standardize this way of problem solving.

Situation 2

The news has been particularly heavy this last week. A recent news story about a racially charged crime has been making the rounds; the community has responded compassionately, and you empathize deeply. You notice that one of your direct reports appears detached; they're usually active and participatory but today feels off. They didn't mention any significant life shifts or milestones in your last one-on-one, nor did they say anything specific this morning. You wonder if it has something to do with the news. You look around and recognize that this person is the only Black person on the floor. What do you do?

Choice A   You reach out via email and tell them that you saw the news. You don't want to assume it's bothering them, but you also want to acknowledge the tragedy. Although there is no official policy around dealing with these kinds of events, you let them know they're able to take time if it feels right to them.

Choice B   Do not mention it. You know processing takes time, and you're unsure how to approach it. You'll revisit this tomorrow and craft a message asking how the employee would like to best use their time.

If You Chose A   Acknowledging can mean a lot to an employee, especially given how taboo it feels to talk about racially charged news. It's not about having the right thing to say as much as it is about recognizing that this might be an emotionally exhausting moment for this person to process. There's no perfect encapsulation of how to address hard things. There is a way to honor someone's experience and process.

If You Chose B   It's okay to give space for someone to process or let the news sit. There is a difference between ignoring something and giving it time. Again, we all process things differently. Some may want the immediate acknowledgment, but it's also okay to give it some space so long as it's something you're doing for your direct report and *not* to make yourself feel comfortable. Frequently, we act in self-interest when we should try and tap into expanding our cultural competency.

Situation 3

Daniela, your teammate, is going through a serious breakup. You run into her in the bathroom and you see her completely sobbing. She sees you and immediately apologizes profusely for crying at work. You understand why she's crying, but this company doesn't appear to be sensitive about emotions, much less to non-work-related emotions. What do you do?

Choice A   You grab tissues. You've been there before. You let her cry until she can't anymore and ask if you can bring her water. Once she's calmer, you ask if she can take the rest of the day off and figure out what you might be able to cover for her.

Choice B   You grab tissues and let her know that she needs to let it all out in the bathroom, so that none of your coworkers see her. You encourage her to cry it out and then pull herself together to finish the rest of the workday. Knowing this work environment, it is better to have her protect herself than to let others see her in this state.

If You Chose A   Empathy is great in these situations. Extend-ing grace to your teammates during tough emotional situations is a great way to both install trust and normalize that life will have twists and turns and it's okay to acknowledge it. It gives your teammate the ability to express her sadness in her own way. Sometimes, those expressions aren't suited for the office or for others. Does she have paid time off (PTO) she can use? Remind her that we don't need to explain why we need PTO and she should use it accordingly! A micro-moment appears here: you're trying to normalize taking breaks or using our time the way we want to.

If You Chose B   You're still expressing empathy but more contained. There's nothing wrong with this—every person deals with and processes life events differently. For you, work-ing is a great distraction. Maybe your teammate finds that she won't be the most productive. Use this to share perspectives around processing tough emotional encounters such as this one. Tap into broadening your cultural competency around how pain and heartbreak may impact other people.

Situation 4

You work at a marketing agency and your client is a consumer-packaged brand. During a call, you discover that you and the client have differing opinions on developing the brand strategy. As you both try to hash out the differences, you sense your client's anger rising. In an attempt to reset the conversation, you ask to regroup. Your client gets angry at the suggestion and begins yelling. Amid your frustration, you start to tear up. What do you do?

Choice A   Internalize your anger and know that you can't fully address this moment. You realize the power dynamics at play and so you let your client continue to yell until the moment is over. You plan to address this with your direct manager.

Choice B   Interject and repeat your next steps to regroup, given high tensions. He might not like it, but you would rather not continue to get yelled at.

If You Choose A   Is there any reason why you feel hesitant to express any type of emotion at this moment? Recall the feeling rules and understand if there were conditioned responses that you had to be mindful of. Also, recognize if anyone else said anything or in defense of you—oftentimes these are great indicators of how your team values emotion.

If You Choose B   It's okay to have boundaries. Yelling isn't a normal reaction. Sometimes, we're conditioned to think that people can talk to us inappropriately and undermine us due to the gender and racial dynamics at play.

Situation 5

It is your annual performance review. Heading into the meeting, you refresh yourself on your accomplishments and areas where you can improve. As you sit with your manager, they go over the standard performance items such as the self-reflection portion and the 360 peer reviews. One of your peer reviews described you as sometimes appearing "disassociated" from work. You're not sure how to receive this, considering you feel like you are present and fairly neutral in most of your work interactions. You want to address this directly with your manager. What do you do?

Choice A   Do nothing. You're not entirely sure what to say or do, given this is the first time you've received this type of feedback on your behavior. You also recognize that you're one of the only people of color in this department and have not heard similar feedback about anyone else. Do you wonder if it's culturally related? How has this work defined what it means to be emotionally acceptable?

Choice B   Follow up to see if that is a consistent thread across all feedback. You question the use of "disassociation" in this context, given that it can hold different meanings in different places. You should feel comfortable asking your manager and understand a bit more of where this feedback stems from. It's also okay to look inward and see if there is something in you that is potentially giving off a sense of indifference.

If You Choose A   Being described as disassociated is tough to process. It is such a strong descriptor and feels hurtful, especially if you don't perceive yourself in that way. It's okay to question the environment and not just question yourself. We find ourselves questioning ourselves based on what people perceive of us, but do we question enough how these perceptions are crafted?

If You Choose B   It's okay to get curious and want more context about feedback. Your manager should be creating a space for you to ask tough questions, especially regarding your performance.

Situation 6

You've been working at a financial firm for more than five years. You've quickly moved up the ranks from associate to manager, faster than anyone else previously in the company. Your manager has reassured you that you are a likely candidate for the director position. In your company's next all-hands meeting, you discover that they have hired a new person to take on the director role. Yes, the role that you thought would be yours. After the meeting, you ask to meet with your manager to gather more information to understand what happened. Your manager simply responds that he has received feedback that you come off as confrontational and, at times, emotional. This is the first you've ever heard of this feedback. What do you do?

Choice A   You ask if your manager can identify clear examples of how you demonstrated being emotional or confrontational. You want to ask your manager how you could have navigated those situations differently. You're angry and disappointed, but you need to know why this happened.

Choice B   You say okay and ask to leave. There's a good chance you are feeling angry and disappointed and the last thing you want to do is be "emotional" after being told that you are.

If You Chose A   More power to you, because I would probably cry. Since you're not me, this highlights a level of emotional maturity that only a few have. I'll also say this, using the term "emotional" can feel completely demeaning, so feeling angry or frustrated is absolutely warranted.

If You Chose B   Hearing that you're emotional is hard, even if it is true. In the workplace context, we see that words can sometimes be weaponized to make us feel less than. It's okay to recognize your humanity and also acknowledge that this work environment is not psychologically or emotionally safe.

Congrats, you made it through all the exercises! How are you feeling? Were you surprised by some of the responses you gravitated toward? Did you learn something new about yourself? Part of being a people manager is that you'll be tasked with dealing with and managing situations that may not have a clear path to resolution. What you can focus on and prepare for is understanding your own set of values and how they'll come into effect given the chance.

Chapter 6|
Offboarding

You enter your first meeting of the day that involves senior leadership. Your team will be presenting the latest customer insights from this past quarter. They have worked hard on this presentation, and you're proud of what they delivered. At the end of the presentation, your senior manager loudly scoffs and says, "That's it?" Your team looks at you bewildered at such a reaction. You're also confused, considering you felt confident about the content. Silence consumes the room. The senior manager continues to harshly critique the presentation and leaves the room when they finish. Your team walks out of the room. You run into a colleague, and you start crying out of frustration, explaining what transpired. Your colleague looks at you with a bit of embarrassment and says something to the effect of, "Hey, you can't let them see you cry!"

I think we can all agree that the above scenario sounds horrible. We're humans at the end of the day, and it is near impossible to suppress feelings during an intense moment, such as being heavily critiqued by a boss. Additionally, in this scenario you've negatively modeled behavior that reinforces that type of feedback is acceptable even at the expense of making the team feel horrendous. The impact of emotional suppression has ripple effects. We've seen this over and over; some of us are currently living in it. While it is undoubtedly doable to manage a business through this lens, employers face the potential for high churn and low morale, which inevitably may lead to a faulty or dissatisfying product or service. All this is to say: shitty feelings can equal shitty results.

If you can believe it, we're at the end of the road of our journey together. Like any good employer would do, it's time for us to conduct an exit interview.

Exit Interview

The purpose of an exit interview is to reflect and gain insight on how to make things better at a workplace. This portion will provide summaries of each section with the associating discussion questions. This interview is intended to help you check in with yourself and how you're feeling, and to reflect on what this journey has been like. What worked? What didn't work? What could be better?

How are you feeling?
This simple question can lead to so much insight about yourself and others. Being in tune with yourself means you have self-awareness and are cognizant of how you act. Are you feeling optimistic? Hopeful? None of these? That's also okay. Change is a process and requires evaluating and reevaluating. Emotion is data. Take a moment and note your breathing and heart rate, and see how your body is at its baseline state.

What has this journey been like for you reading this book and now reflecting on your current workplace?
Did you learn something new? Was everything clear? Do you wish for more?

Do you feel differently about your current workplace?
Did you gain a new perspective on work and how we create culture? Did we share a story or thought that you had not considered?

What do you feel the same about after reading this book?
Are there things you're doing now that are in line with what we shared? Are these things still things you want to keep doing?

What are things you would change about this book?
Are there important steps or realizations that we did not include? If so, how would you explain these ideas to your teammates?

TOO LONG; DIDN'T READ

If you really didn't want to read anything, here are takeaways from each chapter to help inform how you should approach building a more emotional work culture.

Chapter 1: Onboarding

- In order to create space, we should understand the complex collective and individualistic reasons of how we got here.
- Acknowledge that "coming as you are" is only applied to a certain few and understand why that is.
- Gender, race, and socioeconomic dynamics are still in play and can cause people to feel emotionally unsafe.

Chapter 2: Directory, Policies, and Employee Conduct

- In order for us to begin to identify emotions, we have to align on the same baseline emotions that are common in the workplace.
- Reframe positive and negative emotions into "inspiring" and "uninspiring" emotions to normalize the idea that negative feelings are normal because we're humans.
- Recognize the characteristics of an inspiring or uninspiring work culture and how they impact employees and company morale.
- Develop cultural humility to drive awareness and put into context how to help each other out.
- Understand the power of your actions and words. Think about emotional contagion and model behavior.
- Learn how to show accountability through action and not just words.
- Focus on creating policies that set the tone of how to navigate tough situations.

Chapter 3: Benefits Policy

- Simply put, healthy and inspiring work cultures lead to employee retention and creativity.
- When employee retention is high due to company culture, companies see an increase in their bottom line through high productivity.
- Companies can avoid the hidden and not-so-hidden costs of backfilling positions and high turnover rate.
- Great company cultures avoid bad publicity.

Chapter 4: The Catalyst for Change

- The biggest catalyst for change in any work environment is middle management.
- Due to the complex nature of a manager's role, managers are intrinsically well-suited to make work environments inspiring and emotionally nurturing.
- Managers need to be seen as the company culture translators. They bring to life the company values and what the company stands for. However, there are lots of limitations that can prevent this: lack of leadership training, lack of diversity, and more importantly, not being properly trained to manage and regulate employee emotions.

Chapter 5: Career Development

- Dealing with feelings at work can get really sticky—these moments are often unplanned and unexpected. We can reflect and start to form our own internal toolbox that can help us during these times.
- When going through these exercises, recall your initial response to the situation as that tends to tell us more about our attitudes, beliefs, and biases.
- It is important for us to exercise a mindset that welcomes openness and is receptive to the ideals of a compassionate work culture.

Chapter 6: Offboarding

- Get in tune with what comes up for you while reading this book. This is often reflective of how we process work experiences and what we might want to lean into or improve.
- The impact of emotional suppression has ripple effects. Shitty feelings can lead to shitty results. Can we create rewarding and compassionate feelings about work that could result in success?

Conclusion

We can't erase what has been done or said in any of our previous experiences, but I am hopeful that we can make significant, long-lasting changes to how we see and perceive each other. In so many ways, we're just recognizing each other's humanity.

Work culture and feelings are intricately connected. We no longer live in a world where work and home are separate, when in fact they are so closely linked to who we are. We have the power to create incremental change in our everyday lives to create inspiring work cultures. We can build spaces that are considered safe where anyone can come just as they are. By recognizing baseline emotions and developing special skills that allow for folks to begin to develop an awareness of themselves and others, we are creating a tool kit for future managers.

Our society dictates how we should perceive and receive feelings in the workplace. Throughout writing this book, I had to reconcile with a lot of my ideals and the reality we face—it's not going to be fair all the time, companies are not all meritocracies. So many things are out of our control, but I do think we can create meaningful relationships with work and at work. If you're reading this book, you're the reason why.

If you've read everything thus far, I want to thank you. If you skimmed until the end of this page and want the short version of this book, here you go: Just give a shit about yourself and others. I guarantee you all that effort will change things.

Bibliography

Introduction

Nahman, Hayley. "I Asked 1000+ People about Crying at Work and the Answers Are… Emotional." *Repeller*, January 21, 2020. repeller.com/crying-at-work-2/

Chapter 1: Onboarding

Applewhite, Daniel. "Founders and Venture Capital: Racism Is Costing Us Billions." *Forbes*, February 15, 2018. forbes.com/sites/forbesnonprofitcouncil/2018/02/15/founders-and-venture-capital-racism-is-costing-us-billions/?sh=1688180e2e4a

Barsade, Sigal and Olivia A. O'Neill. "Manage Your Emotional Culture: Most Leaders Focus on How Employees Think and Behave—but Feelings Matter Just As Much." *Harvard Business Review*, January/February 2016. hbr.org/2016/01/manage-your-emotional-culture

Brown, Brené. *Atlas of the Heart: Mapping Meaningful Connection and the Language of the Human Spirit.* New York: Random House, 2021.

Chan, Rosalie. "Latinas Feel They Must Work Twice as Hard Survey Says." *Time*, August 15, 2016. time.com/4450710/latinas-business-work-survey-people-en-espanol/

Cohen, Arianne "How Major Life Events iImpact Our Long-Term Wellbeing." *BBC*, September 29, 2020. bbc.com/worklife/article/20200929-how-major-life-events-impact-our-long-term-wellbeing

Côté, Stéphane. "How Social Class Shapes Thoughts and Actions in Organizations." *Research in Organizational Behavior* 31 (2011): 43–71.

Domagalski, Theresa A. "Emotion in Organizations: Main Currents." *Human Relations* 52, no. 6 (June 1999): 833–52. doi.org/10.1177/001872679905200607

Gray, Aysa. "The Bias of 'Professionalism' Standards." *Stanford Social Innovation Review*, June 4, 2019. ssir.org/articles/entry/the_bias_of_professionalism_standards

Groth, Aimee. "Entrepreneurs Don't Have a Special Gene for Risk—
    They Come from Families with Money," *Quartz*, July 17, 2015.
    qz.com/455109/entrepreneurs-dont-have-a-special-gene-for-risk
    -they-come from-families-with-money/

Harvey, Adia. "Are Some Emotions Marked 'Whites Only'? Racialized
    Feeling Rules in Professional Workplaces." *Social Problems* 57,
    no. 2 (May 2010): 251–68.

Horowitz, Ben. *What You Do Is Who You Are: How to Create Your
    Work Culture.* New York: Harper Business, 2019.

Kim, Young-Mee and Sung-il Cho. "Socioeconomic Status, Work-Life
    Conflict, and Mental Health."*American Journal of Industrial
    Medicine* 63, no. 8 (August 2020): 703–12. doi.org/10.1002/ajim.23118

Leading Effectively Staff. "The Importance of Empathy
    in the Workplace." *Center for Creative Leadership*,
    November 28, 2020. ccl.org/articles/leading-effectively-articles/
    empathy-in-the-workplace-a-tool-for-effective-leadership/

Nordhall, Ola and Igor Knez. "Motivation and Justice at Work: The
    Role of Emotion and Cognition Components of Personal and
    Collective Work Identity." *Frontiers in Psychology* 8 (January 15,
    2018): 2307. doi.org/10.3389/fpsyg.2017.02307

O'Hara, Carolyn. "How to Manage an Employee Who's Having a
    Personal Crisis." *Harvard Business Review*, July 5 2018. hbr
    .org/2018/07/how-to-manage-an-employee-whos-having-a-personal-crisis

Thoroughgood, Christian N., Katina B. Sawyer, and Jennica
    R. Webster. "Creating a Trans-Inclusive Workplace: How
    to Make Transgender Employees Feel Valued at Work."
    Harvard Business Review, March/April 2020. hbr.org/2020/03/
    creating-a-trans-inclusive-workplace

Troy, Allison S. et al. "Change the Things You Can: Emotion Regulation
    Is More Beneficial for People from Lower than from Higher
    Socioeconomic Status. *Emotion* 17, no. 1 (2017): 141–54.

Tulshyan, Ruchika. "Return to Office? Some Women of Color Aren't
    Ready," *New York Times*, June 23, 2021. nytimes.com/2021/06/23/us/
    return-to-office-anxiety.html

Walls, Hal. "The Myth of Rationality" (Management). *IIE Solutions* 34,
    no. 12 (December 2012): 18.

Wu, Abby Wen. "The Impact of Race on Mental Health and Well-Being." *Center for Workplace Mental Health*, May 28, 2021. workplacementalhealth.org/News-Events/News-and-Blog/ The-Impact-of-Race-on-Mental-Health-and-Well-being

Xing, Lu, Jian-min (James) Sun, and Denise Jepsen. "Feeling Shame in the Workplace: Examining Negative Feedback as an Antecedent and Performance and Well-Being as Consequences." *Journal of Organizational Behavior* 42, no. 9 (July 28, 2021): 1244–60. doi.org/10.1002/job.2553

Zax, David. "Want to Be Happier at Work? Learn How from These 'Job Crafters,'" *Fast Company*, June 3, 2013. fastcompany.com/3011081/ want-to-be-happier-at-work-learn-how-from-these-job crafters

Zetlin, Minda. "When Trouble at Home Becomes Trouble in the Office." *Inc.*, July 8, 2013. inc.com/minda-zetlin/employee-facing-personal -problems-heres-what-to-do.html

Chapter 2: Directory, Policies, and Employee Code of Conduct

Barsade, Sigal. "Why Fostering a Culture of 'Companionate Love' in the Workplace Matters." *Knowledge at Wharton*, April 2, 2014. knowledge.wharton.upenn.edu/article/fostering-culture-compassion -workplace-matters/

Beck, Julie "Hard Feelings: Science's Struggle to Define Emotions." *Atlantic*, February 24, 2015. theatlantic.com/health/archive/2015/02/ hard-feelings-sciences-struggle-to-define-emotions/385711/

Blankenship, Michael. "The High Cost of Low Morale by Nicole Fink." Roberts Wesleyan College, July 3, 2014. go.roberts.edu/bid/183778/ the-high-cost-of-low-morale-by-nicole-fink

Boroş, Smaranda, Lore van Gorp, and Michael Boiger. "When Holding in Prevents from Reaching Out: Emotion Suppression and Social Support-Seeking in Multicultural Groups." *Frontiers in Psychology* 10 (2019): 2431.

Brown, Brené and Emmanuel Acho. "Brené with Emmanuel Acho on Being Illogical." *Unlocking Us with Brené Brown*, Parcast, April 6, 2122, podcast 62 min. brenebrown.com/podcast/being-illogical/

Carr, Evan W. et al. "The Value of Belonging at Work." *Harvard Business Review*, December 16, 2019. hbr.org/2019/12/ the-value-of-belonging-at-work

Cho, Yoon Jik and Evan J. Ringquist. "Managerial Trustworthiness and Organizational Outcomes." *Journal of Public Administration Research and Theory* 21, no. 1 (2011): 53–86. doi.org/10.1093/jopart/muq015

Crockett, Emily. "The Amazing Tool That Women in the White House Used to Fight Gender Bias." *Vox*, September 14, 2016. vox.com/2016/9/14/12914370/white-house-obama-women-gender-bias-amplification

Dirks, Kurt T., and Donald L. Ferrin. "Trust in Leadership: Meta-Analytic Findings and Implications for Research and Practice." *Journal of Applied Psychology* 87 no. 4 (August 2002): 611–28. doi.org/10.1037/0021-9010.87.4.611

Edmondson, Amy. "Is It Safe to Speak Up at Work? (Transcript)." *WorkLife with Adam Grant*, TED, July 20, 2021. ted.com/podcasts/worklife/is-it-safe-to-speak-up-at-work-transcript

Eldor, Liat. "Public Service Sector: The Compassionate Workplace—The Effect of Compassion and Stress on Employee Engagement, Burnout, and Performance." *Journal of Public Administration Research and Theory* 28, no. (2018): 86–103. doi.org/10.1093/jopart/mux028

Fosslien, Liz and Mollie West Duffy. *No Hard Feelings: The Secret Power of Embracing Emotions at Work*. New York: Portfolio, 2019.

Fredrickson, Barbara L. "The Role of Positive Emotions in Positive Psychology: The Broaden-and-Build Theory of Positive Emotions." *American Psychologist* 56, no. 3 (2001): 218–26. pubmed.ncbi.nlm.nih.gov/11315248/

Haden, Jeff. "Is Your Workplace Toxic? 57 Separate Studies Say Blame Bad Bosses." *Inc*. inc.com/jeff-haden/is-your-workplace-toxic-57-separate-studies-say-blame-bad-bosses.html

Healey, Meghan L. and Murray Grossman. "Cognitive and Affective Perspective-Taking: Evidence for Shared and Dissociable Anatomical Substrates." *Frontiers in Neurology* 9 (2018): 491.

Johnson, Matthew Kuan. "Joy: A Review of the Literature and Suggestions for Future Directions." *The Journal of Positive Psychology* 15, no. 1 (2020): 5–24. doi.org/10.1080/17439760.2019.1685581

Kelley, James. *The Crucible's Gift: 5 Lessons From Authentic Leaders Who Thrive in Adversity*. Vancouver, WA: Executives After Hours, 2018.

Ladika, Susan. "The Value of Trust." *HR Magazine*, June 1, 2021. shrm .org/hr-today/news/hr-magazine/summer2021/pages/the-value-of-trust.aspx

Lau, Yolanda. "Bringing Emotions into the Workplace." *Forbes*, May 6, 2020. forbes.com/sites/forbeshumanresourcescouncil/2020/05/06/ bringing-emotions-into-the-workplace/

Lekas, Helen-Maria, Kerstin Pahl, and Crystal Fuller Lewis. "Rethinking Cultural Competence: Shifting to Cultural Humility." *Health Services Insights* 13 (January 2020). doi.org/10.1177/1178632920970580

Madera, Juan M., Jack A. Neal, and Mary Dawson. "A Strategy for Diversity Training: Focusing on Empathy in the Workplace." *Journal of Hospitality & Tourism Research* 35, no. 4 (November 2011): 469–87.

Mayer, Roger C., James H. Davis, and F. David Schoorman. "An Integrative Model of Organizational Trust." *The Academy of Management Review* 20, no. 3 (July 1995): 709–34.

Meanwell, Emily, Joseph D. Wolfe, and Tim Hallett. "Old Paths and New Directions: Studying Emotions in the Workplace." *Sociology Compass* 2, no. 2 (2008): 537–59. compass.onlinelibrary.wiley.com/ doi/10.1111/j.1751-9020.2007.00077.x

Moller, Arlen C., Edward L. Deci, and Andrew J. Elliot. "Person-Level Relatedness and the Incremental Value of Relating." *Personality & Social Psychology Bulletin* 36, no. 6 (2010): 754–67. doi:10.1177/0146167210371622

Nielson, Nicolai Chen, Gemma D'Auria, and Sasha Zolley. "Tuning In, Turning Outward: Cultivating Compassionate Leadership in a Crisis." *Mckinsey*, May 1, 2020. mckinsey.com/ capabilities/people-and-organizational-performance/our-insights/ tuning-in-turning-outward-cultivating-compassionate-leadership-in-a-crisis

Pearson, Christine M. "The Smart Way to Respond to Negative Emotions at Work." *MIT Sloan Management Review*, Spring 2017. sloanreview.mit.edu/article/the-smart-way-to-respond-to-negative -emotions-at-work/

Pir, Sesil. "8 Mindsets That Will Re-Shape the Future of Work Experience,." *Forbes*, March 28, 2021. forbes.com/sites/sesilpir/2021/03/28/8-mindsets-that-will-re-shape-the-future-of-work-experience/

Psychology Today Staff. "Adlerian Therapy." *Psychology Today*, last updated April 4, 2022. psychologytoday.com/us/therapy-types/adlerian-therapy

Rousseau, Denise M. et al. "Not So Different After All: A Cross-Discipline View of Trust." *The Academy of Management Review* 23, no. 3 (July 1998): 393–404.

Rozovsky, Julia. "The Five Keys to a Successful Google Team." *re:Work*, November 17, 2015. rework.withgoogle.com/blog/five-keys-to-a-successful-google-team/

Santos, Laurie. "Emotions are Data…So Listen to Them." *The Happiness Lab with Dr. Laurie Santos*, Pushkin Industries, January 3, 2022, podcast 45:03. pushkin.fm/podcasts/the-happiness-lab-with-dr-laurie-santos/emotions-are-data-so-listen-to-them

Scott, Kim. *Just Work: How to Root Out Bias, Prejudice, and Bullying to Build a Kick-Ass Culture of Inclusivity.* New York: St. Martin's Press, 2021.

Scott, Kim. *Radical Candor: Be a Kick-Ass Boss Without Losing Your Humanity.* New York: St. Martin's Press, 2017.

Sineck, Simon. *Start with Why: How Great Leaders Inspire Everyone to Take Action.* New York: Portfolio, 2009.

Timms, Michael "Blame Culture Is Toxic. Here's How to Stop It." *Harvard Business Review*, February 9, 2022. hbr.org/2022/02/blame-culture-is-toxic-heres-how-to-stop-it

Whitney-Coulter, Ava. "Brené Brown on What It Really Means to Trust." *Mindful*, February 5, 2021. mindful.org/brene-brown-on-what-it-really-means-to-trust/

Zak, Paul J. "The Neuroscience of Trust: Management Behaviors That Foster Employee Engagement." *Harvard Business Review*, January/February 2017. hbr.org/2017/01/the-neuroscience-of-trust

Chapter 3: Benefits Policy

Cantor, Rachel. "My Unfiltered Thoughts On: The Great Jones Cofounder Fallout." *Sidekick*, July 1, 2021. morningbrew.com/sidekick/stories/2021/07/01/unfiltered-thoughts-great-jones-cofounder-fallout

Deloitte Staff. *Inclusive Mobility: How Mobilizing a Diverse Workforce Can Drive Business Performance*. London: Deloitte Development LLC, 2018. deloitte.com/us/en/pages/tax/articles/inclusive-mobility-diverse-workforce-drive-business-performance.html

Gurchiek, Kathy. "Survey: Workplace Friends Important Retention Factor." SHRM, December 16, 2014. shrm.org/resourcesandtools/hr-topics/employee-relations/pages/workplace-friendships.aspx

Parke, Michael. "All the Feels: How Companies Can Benefit from Employees' Emotions." *Knowledge at Wharton*, September 7, 20201. businessamlive.com/all-the-feels-how-companies-can-benefit-from-employees-emotions/

Robbin, Scoty and Ed O'Boyle. "The Business Impact of Human Emotions." Gallup, November 1, 2012. news.gallup.com/businessjournal/158450/business-impact-human-emotions.aspx

Scheff, Sue. "How Negative Publicity (Shaming) Can Impact Your Company and More." *Huffington Post*, July 20, 2017. huffpost.com/entry/how-negative-publicity-shaming-can-impact-your-company_b_596d2279e4b05561da5a59ca

Seppälä, Emma and Kim Cameron. "Proof That Positive Work Cultures Are More Productive." *Harvard Business Review*, December 1, 2015. hbr.org/2015/12/proof-that-positive-work-cultures-are-more-productive

Chapter 4: The Catalyst for Change

Hancock, Bryan and Bill Schaninger. "The Vanishing Middle Manager." *McKinsey Talks Talent*, McKinsey & Company, February 5, 2021, podcast 28:44. mckinsey.com/capabilities/people-and-organizational-performance/our-insights/the-vanishing-middle-manager

Miller, Scott. *Everyone Deserves a Great Manager: The 6 Critical Practices for Leading a Team*. New York: Simon & Schuster, 2019.

Scott, Kim. "Radical Candor 101." *Radical Candor*. radicalcandor.com/
frequently-asked questions/

U.S. Bureau of Labor Statistics. "Household Data Annual Averages:
11. Employed Persons by Detailed Occupation, Sex, Race, and
Hispanic or Latino Ethnicity." Last modified January 22, 2022.
bls.gov/cps/cpsaat11.htm

Working with Feelings: Caring for Your Employees
Through Cultural Humility and Emotional Fluency
Isidora Torres

ISBN 979-8-218-11427-5

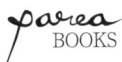

pavea
BOOKS

Published by Parea Books
www.pareabooks.com
about@pareabooks.com

EDITOR
Alyea Canada

PROOFREADER
Janet Blake

DESIGN
Frances Baca and Noah Venezia

ILLUSTRATION
Bria Benjamin

Typeset in Union and TT Livret
Printed in Canada

MIX
Paper from
responsible sources
FSC
www.fsc.org   FSC® C016245